NAMAHAGE

Guardians of Northern Japan

Anthony DiCristofano

Copyright © 2025 Anthony P. DiCristofano

All rights reserved. No part of this book may be reproduced, stored in a retrieval system, or transmitted in any form or by any means, electronic, mechanical, photocopying, recording, or otherwise, without the prior written permission of the publisher, except in the case of brief quotations embodied in reviews or scholarly articles.

This is a work of nonfiction. Every reasonable effort has been made to ensure the accuracy and integrity of the information presented.
Printed in the United States of America.

ISBN: 979-8-9995181-5-6

Cover design, interior formatting, and illustrations by the author.

Table of Contents

CHAPTER 1: The Mask at the Threshold

CHAPTER 2: The Oga Peninsula: Landscape and Winter

CHAPTER 3: Origins and Etymology

CHAPTER 4: The Masks: Faces of Fear

CHAPTER 5: The Ritual Garb: Straw and Embodiment

CHAPTER 6: Implements of Authority

CHAPTER 7: The Visit: A Night of Fear

CHAPTER 8: The Necessity of Fear

CHAPTER 9: The Communal Frame: Order and Obligation

CHAPTER 10: Other Demons at the Door

CHAPTER 11: From Ritual to Performance and Icon

CHAPTER 12: Ethnographic Voices

CHAPTER 13: The Lasting Image

CHAPTER 1:
The Mask at the Threshold

「悪い子はいねが！」
Warui ko wa inē ga!
Are there any bad children here?

    The first thing is the door. It quivers once, then again, as if a hand outside is testing the house to see what it is made of. A child's breath stalls. The lamp fusses with its own flame. Straw rubs wood. A voice comes through the seam, flattened by the plank but still enormous.

「泣く子はいねが！」
Naku ko wa inega!
"Any crybabies here?"

    No museum glass stands between the voice and the room. There is no stage, no usher, no kindly narrator to explain what you are hearing. There is only the door, the cold pressing at its edges, and the fact that someone on the other side wants to know whether you have been lazy.

    The knock comes again. Not polite. Not cruel. Inevitable. The father moves first, because someone must. The latch is a simple iron hook that has worked for decades without drama. It lifts with the small scrape of metal on metal that a household can recognize in the dark. The door opens enough to let the cold lean inside, enough to suggest the outline of something waiting. The house holds still. A horn glints, a mouth of carved wood breathes, and the straw at the edge of the threshold stirs as if alive. Nothing more is needed. The presence at the door has declared itself, and the family knows who has come.

    What you have just felt is not a tale about long-ago villagers or an imported Halloween. It is a living custom from the Oga Peninsula in northern Akita Prefecture, enacted each winter in real homes with real children who cry and then straighten, and with parents who bow, joke, bargain, and remember. The visitors are called Namahage. They are not actors in a theme park. They are not docents. They are neighbors wearing carved faces and straw coats who arrive to do a job that the village decided long ago must be done with volume.

The Namahage ask questions that are simple on purpose. Have you studied? Have you helped? Have you obeyed? They are not interested in nuance. Nuance is what bends planks, rots rope, loosens the small ties that hold a household together when the wind rises and the road vanishes under snow. The Namahage are there to scrape off softness. The word itself carries the scrape: nama for the blistered skin that forms when you sit too close to the fire, hage for peeling it away. Laziness made into a surface. Discipline made into a hand.

This book begins at that door because everything that follows starts there. Masks, straw, origin myths, dialect, craft, tourism, shame, survival, comparison to other winter beasts: none of it matters if you cannot hear the knock and feel the latch in your palm. I can give you etymologies and dates, quote pamphlets and papers, point at photographs of painted eyes and matted sleeves. Useful. Necessary. But the heart of it is the room. A child who will remember tonight for fifty years. A mother who cannot decide whether to smile to steady the children or keep her mouth still in respect. A father whose voice drops half an octave because a different voice has entered his house and he must answer it.

Namahage is under-described in English except as a festival. Guides tell you where to stand to watch. Hotels print schedules. There are postcards and posters and cheerful mascots. The staged version has its place. It keeps the shape of the thing visible and pays for the upkeep of masks. But if you only see the performance hall, you will miss the substance. The substance is private. No ticket. No program. The Namahage do not stay on a platform. They step into kitchens and genkan (entryway), and they speak names.

Ritualized fear is the engine here. Not panic. Not trauma that shatters and stays in shards. Fear with a border and a calendar. Fear that arrives, does its work, and departs, leaving an outline that people trace for the rest of their lives when they need to remember what is expected of them. We moderns like to tell ourselves that reason persuades. Sometimes it does. Often it drifts. Fear works where reason fails. Not the fear of a tyrant or a household bully. The fear given shape by the community and kept on a leash by the community, pointed inward for one night so that it does not leak into every other night.

If you grew up far from snowbound Akita, you still know the pattern. Humans everywhere invite something frightening to visit and to teach. In Austria it rattles chains. In Bulgaria it stamps bells into the road. In Sardinia it wears a blackened face and moves with the weight of a century under its hide. In America, we turned the door ritual into a sugar economy and a parade of costumes. Different masks. Same hunger. We have always needed a figure to knock and ask whether we have done the work.

Japan is often described as a culture of shame rather than guilt, and there is a whole literature that tries to turn that sentence into a map. We will come to that. For now, notice the architecture of the night. The accusations are asked as questions. The children are not privately scolded but publicly addressed within the smallest public there is: the family. The parents are required to defend. They pour, bow, promise. The house becomes a small court where everyone knows the verdict in advance and speaks it aloud anyway so that it will have weight. Shame by itself can be poisonous. Shame turned into ritual can be medicine.

This is not gentle. That is the point. Traditions that survive often do so because they are useful and a little terrifying. A community that lives with hard winters will make hard customs if those customs keep people attentive. The Oga coastline teaches this lesson every year. Snow pins doors. The sea gives and takes without apology. Rice grows if you attend to it. Boats return if you respect limits. In such a place, a soft heart is not a virtue. It is a hazard. The Namahage are the hazard made safe and temporary. A threat borrowed from the world, dressed in straw, and brought to the hearth for one appointed hour.

What follows in these pages is not an academic catalogue and not a collection of spooky stories. It is a guided walk from the threshold into the rooms the ritual touches. We will look at the masks: carved from wood, painted in primary colors that read across a smoky room, eyes widened to glare even when the lamp is low. We will look at the straw: the mino coat that changes the outline of the human underneath, that hisses when it rubs the doorframe, that drops a field onto the floor with every shrug. We will walk through the sequence of a visit from beginning to end, with all the choreography that hides inside the noise. We will set the ritual inside its landscape and its history, where gods and ogres blur into each other the way snow and sea do at the horizon. We will put Oga in conversation with other winter visitors from far away, then we will ask the questions that matter most: what does this fear do, who does it serve, why do people who could stop it choose not to.

This account comes from study, firsthand observation, and long respect for how living traditions endure pressure. I've read and listened to those who grew up with the knock, traced the arguments over meaning and change, and watched how modern life strains but never erases these forms. My aim is not to reduce the Namahage to folklore or spectacle, but to let the ritual do what it does even on the page: demand, correct, endure.

A caution early on: authenticity is not a fossil. The Namahage you will meet in these chapters are many things at once. They are divine visitors in some tellings. They are demons in others. They are the boys from down the lane under the straw, growing into men by learning to scare the children they once were. They are also, on other nights in other places, a show for cameras and a line item on a tourist brochure. None of these versions cancels the others. Communities preserve what they need by adapting what they must. If you want purity, you will miss the living thing.

Return to the door for a moment. The child is still in the mother's elbow. The father still holds the latch. The voice is still asking the same question it asked last year and the year before that. You can learn every origin story, climb every stone stair that locals say ogres built in a night, memorize every line of dialect, and still, the truth sits in the bones of the house when the knock lands. Ritual is not an idea. It is a sound, a temperature, a practiced exchange.

Open the door a hand's breadth. Enough to see an eye cut from wood and painted to show too much white. Enough to feel the breath of winter come in and make the lamp kneel for a moment. Enough to hear the line that a thousand households know by heart.

「怠け者はいねが！」
Namake-mono wa inega!
"Any lazy ones here?"

Close it again. We will open it fully later. First we will step outside and look back at the land that makes a threshold feel like a moral device. A peninsula that juts into a harsh sea. Villages that must organize themselves to outlast weather. Fields that ask for human hands when human hands might prefer a brazier and a nap. In the next chapter, we will stand on that coast and watch the snow push inland and see how isolation grows roots for stories. For now, the image is enough.

The mask waits. The straw drips. The house keeps its breath steady by counting. Somewhere down the lane another door answers the knock. The year is about to turn. The visitors are at the threshold. And whether you grew up in Oga or in a place where winter never learns your name, you know what it means for a community to summon a fear, invite it inside, and ask it to help raise its children.

「また来るぞ。」

Mata kuru zo.

We will come again.

CHAPTER 2: The Oga Peninsula: Landscape and Winter

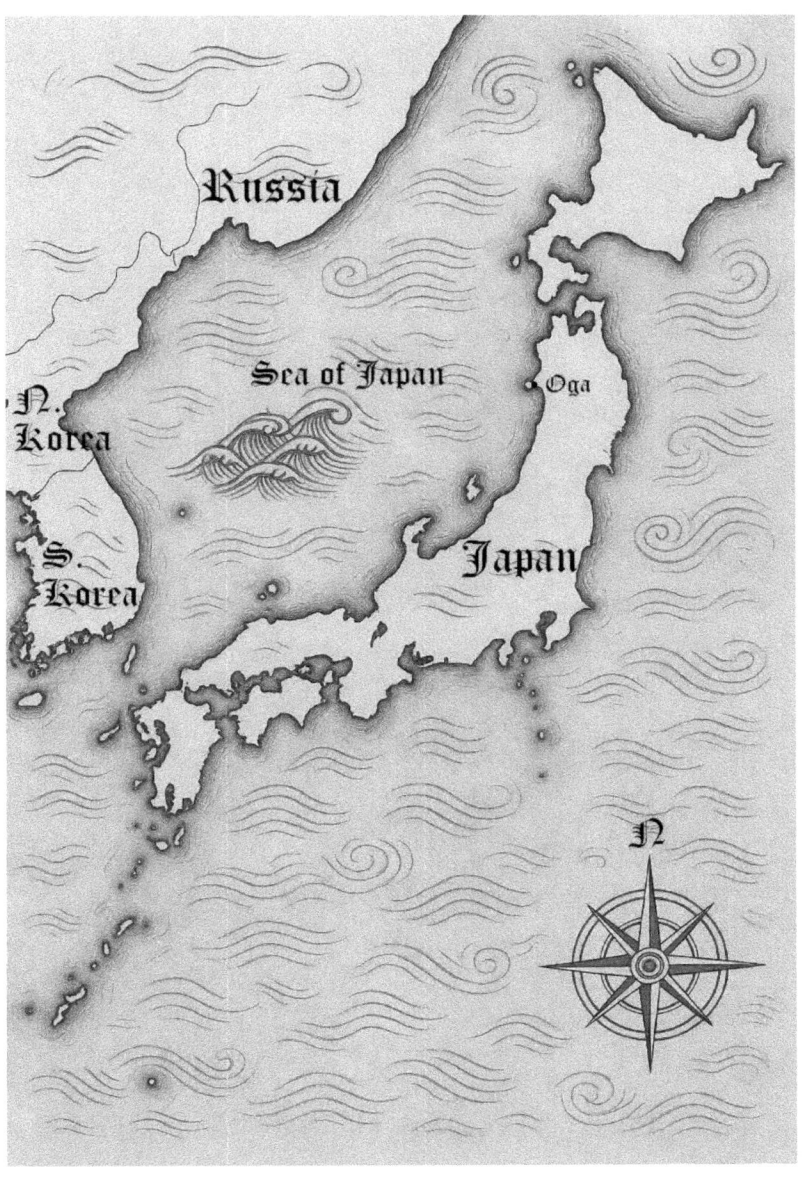

Section 1: Geography & Atmosphere

Stand on a winter headland of the Oga Peninsula and you understand why people here imagine demons. The Sea of Japan does not roll or lap. It hammers. In January, waves crash against the black volcanic rocks, throwing spray into the air that the wind drives back in stinging sheets of salt water. Gulls wheel above the cliffs, their cries thin against the thunder of surf. The wind cuts straight through coats, numbs fingers in minutes, and makes every breath sharp with cold. Snow does not drift down gently but lashes sideways, carried hard by gusts that strip warmth and vision alike.

The peninsula juts from Akita Prefecture like a clenched fist into the sea. To its west lies only open water, the Russian coast far beyond the horizon. To its east stretch the rice fields and forests of Tōhoku, blanketed in white half the year. Oga is not central, not metropolitan, not on the way to anywhere else. It is an edge. In Japan, edges mean survival by self-reliance. Roads vanish in storms. Ferries stop. Villages live on what they have and on what they can wring from the coast.

Winter here is not a postcard. It is not the aesthetic dusting of snow that city people photograph under lanterns. It is depth, three to four meters of it each year, stacked against doors, erasing paths, bending telephone poles, sealing homes. In some winters, drifts swallow the first floor of a house so that families dig tunnels to daylight. Farmers stack firewood in October knowing every log will be gone by March. Fishermen pray to whatever god listens over the roar of surf before they push boats into black water. The environment does not care if you believe in gods or demons. It asks only if you worked hard enough.

Summer is no reprieve. Heat brings sweat, insects, sudden storms. Rice paddies stretch like mirrors, demanding labor in bent posture from sunup to sundown. A single missed day can ruin a crop. A single storm can flood fields, undoing months of work. The sea is generous with fish but never safe. Men disappear on calm mornings when the horizon looks smooth as lacquer, their boats found days later broken and adrift.

This is the soil where Namahage grew. Not a playful invention, not entertainment. A practice with consequences, born in a place where being unprepared for winter could kill. If your children sat too long by the brazier, if your wife left work undone, if your husband skipped his duty to the nets, the penalty was not scolding. It was hunger, exposure, loss. Discipline was not an option. It was the only insurance policy.

Geography here is more than backdrop, it is script. The mountains rise like shoulders against the sky, heavy with cedar and pine. They seem close enough to lean on the villages below. Roads cut through them in hairpin turns, but when the snow comes, those roads may as well not exist. Isolation is enforced not by choice but by nature. The rest of Japan recedes. What remains is the small circle of the village, the sea at its edge, the mountain at its back, and the weather pressing from above. Within that circle, rituals flourish because they are needed.

Isolation preserves. In Tokyo, modernity erodes customs by sheer pace. In Oga, modernity arrives late, sometimes reluctantly. Old dialects linger. Festivals resist dilution. Strangers stand out. In some hamlets, words survive that even Akita City residents no longer use. What looks like remoteness to outsiders is, for locals, continuity. The Namahage survive here because the land keeps them alive.

In summer, the same mountains that shield become heavy with insects, their streams feeding terraced paddies. The air smells of wet earth and growing grain. But even in this season of green, villagers know winter is waiting. The contrast sharpens awareness. A hot day in August carries the knowledge that January will arrive like a creditor collecting its due. Perhaps this is why the Namahage demand diligence at the turning of the year, because in places like Oga, every season is only the shadow of the next.

The peninsula does not offer spectacle the way Kyoto offers temples or Tokyo offers towers. It offers endurance. The coastline is raw. Fishing villages cling to the waterline, roofs heavy with snow guards. Fields tilt upward into forest where shrines hide under cedar boughs. Paths vanish quickly into drifts or undergrowth. It is the kind of land where one does not expect visitors. That is precisely why the idea of visitors, masked, horned, roaring at your threshold, takes root so naturally.

Demons here are not exotic intruders. They are the weather given a face. They are the mountains stepping into your house. You can call them gods, ogres, spirits, or neighbors in disguise. It doesn't matter. What matters is that the land itself feels capable of pounding on your door, demanding to know if you worked hard enough to deserve tomorrow.

To understand Namahage, you have to feel this peninsula first. You have to imagine yourself in a village where the road disappears and the horizon is only snow and sea. You have to imagine a year where slackness means hunger. You have to imagine a culture where the line between superstition and survival is not clear, and where a mask at the door is not only theater but instruction.

Oga is not central Japan. It is marginal Japan, peripheral, out at the edge. And yet that is where rituals like this survive best. In the capital, demons become mascots. At the edge, demons stay demons. They are kept alive not by nostalgia but by need.

Stand again on the headland. The wind is a lash. The sea keeps pounding. A village crouches against the shore, houses huddled shoulder to shoulder as if warmth could be shared through walls. Inside those houses, families bank fires, prepare sake, and wait for a knock they know will come. The land has already given them its orders. The Namahage are only here to remind them.

Section 2: Hard Life, Hard Traditions

If the land of Oga is a fist thrust into the sea, life upon it has always been lived with clenched teeth. Survival here was not a given but an achievement. To live through winter required planning, discipline, and a kind of stubbornness that could be mistaken for faith.

The Oga Peninsula has never been wealthy. Its soil is thin, its growing season short, and its coastline, while abundant with fish, is punishing. Rice, the heart of the Japanese table, grows reluctantly here. Families maintained narrow paddies carved from sloping fields and depended on every stalk. A harvest lost to storm or blight meant not inconvenience but hunger. Stored grain determined whether households endured until spring.

Fishing gave a second lifeline, but the sea took as much as it gave. The Sea of Japan is notorious for sudden squalls. A calm horizon in the morning could become a storm wall by afternoon. Fatal accidents still occur on this coast, and in older centuries, boats vanished without a trace. Villages held ceremonies for men lost at sea in numbers that would stagger outsiders. It is no coincidence that shrines along the coast are built stout and low, their roofs angled to shed snow and their altars heavy with offerings to placate the sea.

Life inland was no easier. Firewood was currency in winter. Families cut and stacked cedar and pine through summer, knowing the piles must last until March or April. A miscalculation could mean weeks of smoke-thin fires, rooms where frost rimed the tatami, children waking with breath visible in the air. Cattle and horses had to be fed from the same meager stores. Tools broke under ice. Roofs groaned under snow weight, collapsing if neglected.

This hardship bred customs that were never decorative. Every ritual, every communal act, carried a practical function. Oga's people learned that survival required not only individual effort but communal enforcement of effort. One family's laziness could ripple into the whole village: an uncle who shirked his turn at net mending meant fewer fish for everyone, a child who refused lessons meant a weaker hand in the fields years later. Isolation magnified the consequences. There were no reserves to draw from, no distant markets to bail out negligence.

The traditions existed because life itself carried stakes, farming, storms, and hunger made consequences unavoidable. They were reminders, warnings, and sometimes threats. The Namahage are the most famous, but they are only one expression of a deeper cultural reflex: to externalize discipline, to make it visible, audible, and communal. If the land demanded vigilance, the people turned that demand into ritual.

In Akita, winter dictated behavior. Japanese records from the Edo period describe Akita's winters as among the harshest in the archipelago. Reports sent to the shogunate catalogued food shortages and heavy snow that made transport impossible. Even today, Akita Prefecture is designated part of the "Gosetsu chitai," Japan's heavy snow belt. The term is not poetic; it is a government classification acknowledging the economic and logistical challenges of snowfall measured in meters.

In Oga, this meant months when roads disappeared, fields lay dormant, and families huddled in one-room homes heated by a single hearth. It also meant months when work could not be ignored. Idle bodies stiffened, idle minds brooded, idle children became careless. To sit too close to the brazier without purpose gave rise to the word that became the very name of the demons: namomi, the heat blisters of laziness. The tradition of scraping them away was not metaphorical indulgence. It was a moral directive.

The villagers did not have the luxury of ignoring slackness. The snow was a kind of judge, recording who had prepared and who had not. A man who split extra wood was remembered. A family that ran out of rice was marked. The Namahage's annual visit, with its roaring accusations, was only the ritualized voice of what the snow already said in silence. In Oga, communal responsibility hardened into enforcement. Villages had to ensure that every member carried weight. A single family's weakness could endanger the whole. If one household failed to keep dikes in repair, paddies downstream flooded. If one fisherman neglected his share of rope-making, nets tore and the catch dwindled. The community bore the cost of individual negligence.

Thus discipline became theatrical. It was not enough for parents to quietly scold children, or for neighbors to gossip about idleness. The correction had to be embodied, given sound and force, so that no one could pretend they had not heard. The Namahage fulfilled this role, but so did other practices: public work days where attendance was not optional, village councils where promises were spoken aloud, even seasonal festivals where offerings were made not only to gods but to each other, as a demonstration that one was pulling his share.

Children grew up in this system understanding that fear was not cruelty but instruction. They learned early that the village watched as surely as the sea. To modern sensibilities this may appear harsh, but in context it was essential. Survival in Oga was not a private project. It was a collective wager against winter, and rituals were the insurance payments.

The same rule that governed discipline also shaped worship. Shinto shrines dot the peninsula, some no larger than a single wooden alcove, others substantial structures at the base of mountains. They mark fishing grounds, farming fields, and crossroads where travelers might pray for safe passage. To outsiders they suggest piety; to villagers they signaled obligation. Offerings were less about abstract devotion and more about balance: if the sea took, the sea must also be placated; if the field yielded, the field must also be thanked.

Buddhism, too, left its traces here, carried from larger cities into the countryside. But in Oga it was Shinto's local, place-bound spirits that mattered most. The mountain above your house could kill you in an avalanche. The bay below could swallow a father whole. Better to acknowledge those powers than to imagine oneself immune.

It was within this web of necessity that the Namahage took their place. They were not rivals to shrines or priests; they were reminders of the same truths: survival requires effort and neglect brings consequence. The gods might protect, the ancestors might guide, but the demons made sure you remembered your duty that night.

Many rural regions of Japan have preserved rituals, but Oga's are particularly stark. Elsewhere, folk dances celebrate harvest, fertility, or marriage. In Oga, the most famous tradition storms into homes demanding proof of labor. The difference reflects the peninsula's conditions. Soft traditions do not survive hard climates.

Even the costuming of Namahage reflects agricultural reality. The straw coats they wear are not symbolic abstractions but garments once used in the fields to shed rain and snow. The sound of straw in a doorway was not an invention. It was the echo of fields, of labor woven into clothing, now carried into the home as reminder.

The masks, too, are not merely art. Their exaggerated features, such as jagged teeth, gaping mouths, and eyes wide with painted whites, mirror the storms that batter the coast. A child staring into those eyes sees not only a demon but the weather itself, the same force that drives fathers out to sea and buries barns under snow.

Traditions endure because they serve. In Oga, the Namahage survive not as quaint folklore but because they speak to the core logic of the place: discipline enforced through fear, fear bounded by ritual. They are not entertainment. They are continuity.

A ritual this harsh could not last if it were only cruelty. It lasts because it works. Parents find their authority reinforced, children learn boundaries, the village shares a collective reminder that laziness is dangerous. Outsiders may see only theatrics, but insiders understand the efficiency. A shouted command in straw and wood can do the work of months of quiet correction.

And so the tradition has never been ornamental. It has been functional. To understand it, one must first understand the peninsula that required such a tool: a land where winters cut deep, where the sea took men without warning, and where survival depended on every hand keeping its promise.

Section 3: Isolation & Preservation

To understand why Namahage survived into the twenty-first century, you must understand what it means to live at the margins. Oga, unlike the larger, centralized metropolitan areas of Japan, has never been a hub of politics or fashion. It is a peninsula set apart, a landscape that folds its people inward and teaches them to measure time by seasons instead of calendars. In such places, customs do not vanish quickly. They settle into the soil.

Isolation is not only geographical. It is cultural. In the centuries when Japan's main islands were drawn into national networks of roads, trade, and railways, Oga remained stubbornly peripheral. Until the late nineteenth century, reliable routes into the peninsula were coastal, by boat. Inland tracks often disappeared under snow half the year, and even when clear, they were slow and dangerous. The Meiji government modernized ports and railroads in Akita City, but Oga lagged behind, too small and rugged to attract significant investment. By the time Japan was turning toward industrial expansion, Oga was still living at the pace of fishing nets and rice paddies.

This distance insulated traditions. Villages repeated their cycles with little interruption from outside tastes. Dialects thickened, songs retained older words, and festivals kept their teeth. Where more connected regions softened rituals into pageantry, Oga preserved their rough edges. In urban Japan, many seasonal customs became performative floats pulled in parades, masked dances performed on stages. In Oga, the masks still entered houses. The difference was not about stubbornness for its own sake but about necessity. A village without outside supply chains could not afford to relax its cultural tools of discipline.

Anthropologists have long noted that "peripheral" regions often safeguard "core" practices. Customs that seem archaic or theatrical to outsiders are preserved because they remain useful. In Oga, Namahage kept its authority precisely because the community was small enough, and closed enough, that the visit mattered to every household. No one could pretend they were exempt. No one could say the demons did not come to their door.

The size of Oga's population reinforced this continuity. Today the entire peninsula counts fewer than thirty thousand residents, spread across fishing villages and farming hamlets. In earlier centuries, the numbers were not much higher. Communities were intimate enough that reputations lasted a lifetime. A child who trembled under the Namahage's mask grew into an adult who remembered that terror when raising his own children. When it was his turn to don the straw coat, he brought with him the memory of fear and the understanding of its purpose. In this way, the ritual recycled itself generation after generation, not as abstract folklore but as lived memory.

Isolation also meant that Oga's people had little choice but to value what they inherited. In a metropolis, new fashions arrive constantly, offering alternatives to old ways. In Oga, alternatives were scarce. The sea offered no distraction. The mountains offered no escape. Rituals became anchors in a landscape that otherwise shifted only with weather. To abandon them would be to invite disorder, to leave behind the only tools the community trusted to maintain cohesion.

This insulation gave the Namahage another advantage: ambiguity. In urban Japan, where rituals were increasingly subject to outside observation, practices became standardized and codified, their meanings written down for audiences. In Oga, meanings remained layered and flexible. The Namahage could be demons one year, gods the next, depending on which elder was telling the story or which household carried which memory. This fluidity made the custom resilient. Without outside pressure to define itself too narrowly, it could adapt to each generation without losing its core.

There is a paradox here. Isolation both preserved and exposed. It preserved because it shielded Oga from modernization's constant churn. It exposed because it left villages vulnerable to the full weight of winter and sea. The Namahage embodied both sides. They were preserved as a ritual because isolation demanded continuity. They were terrifying because exposure demanded discipline.

In the twentieth century, even as railways reached Akita Prefecture and national media began to broadcast new images of modern Japan, Oga remained, in many ways, outside the current. Photographs from the 1950s show children in woolen coats pressed against walls while straw-clad figures thunder into their homes. These are not staged images for tourists. They are local records, memories fixed on film. While cities filled their calendars with neon and cinema, Oga still filled its nights with masks and horns.

The persistence of Namahage demonstrates a broader truth about culture: what survives is not necessarily what is most beautiful or most benign, but what is most needed. Songs of harvest may fade when tractors arrive. Costumes of courtship may disappear when marriage customs shift. But a ritual that disciplines children and reinforces communal responsibility, that remains useful as long as survival depends on vigilance.

Today, Oga faces the same pressures that rural communities across Japan endure: depopulation, aging, and the pull of urban life. Young people leave for universities in Tokyo or Sendai and often do not return. Villages shrink. Yet even in this thinning, the Namahage remain. In fact, the ritual has become more visible precisely because it is threatened. Preservation societies now maintain the masks, and the tradition is showcased for visitors. But in Oga's homes on New Year's Eve, the private version still continues. Children still hear the pounding on the door. Parents still bow and promise improvement. The ritual still binds the community, however small, in the same shared fear that bound their ancestors.

This endurance is not nostalgia. It is adaptation. Oga has always known isolation. It has always known how to protect what matters by keeping it close. The Namahage are proof. They endure not because they are quaint but because they still speak to the fundamental condition of life on the peninsula: hardship met with discipline, and discipline carried forward through ritual.

The lesson is broader than Oga. Isolation is not only physical distance. It is also a state of mind. Communities everywhere, when cut off, by geography, poverty, or circumstance, tend to preserve the tools that enforce cohesion. For Oga, that tool is the Namahage. It is a mask that has walked through centuries of storms and scarcity without losing its voice.

In the end, the peninsula's remoteness is not a weakness. It is a forge. It has burned away the ornamental and left only what could endure. The Namahage are one of those enduring things. They remain because they are still needed, because isolation sharpened them into instruments too practical to discard.

Section 4: Foreshadowing the Namahage

Before the Namahage appear in masks and straw, they exist in the land itself. The Oga Peninsula is already a stage set for visitation. The mountains stand like watchmen, cedar groves whisper in winter wind, and the sea strikes with a rhythm that feels closer to speech than to sound. When villagers imagined demons coming down from the peaks or gods arriving from across the water, they were not inventing out of nothing. They were reading the landscape as text.

Snow is the first mask. It falls without pause, soft but relentless, covering paths, softening corners, erasing landmarks. By January, the world is unrecognizable. A man can leave his own house and struggle to find it again in the whiteout. A child stepping into the lane disappears after a dozen paces, swallowed by drifts. To live in such a world is to know that ordinary things can transform into something alien overnight. If snow can turn a familiar street into an uncharted expanse, why should it not also turn a neighbor into a demon when the year turns?

The sea is another mask. By day it glitters, and boats move across it with the ease of habit. By night it becomes black glass, without boundary or measure. Fishermen have always said that the sea has moods, but on this coast those moods are violent. Storms rise without warning, swallowing boats whole. To the villagers, the sea was not a backdrop but a presence, powerful and unpredictable. To imagine it embodied as a horned figure striding through the doorway is less a leap of faith than a natural extension of lived experience.

The mountains complete the triad. Dense cedar forests rise up the slopes, their trunks dark, their crowns heavy with snow. The air is different there: muffled, resinous, steeped in shadow. Folklore across Japan has long associated mountains with spirits, both protective and dangerous. On Oga, the boundary between village and mountain is narrow. Farmers worked at the edge of the forest. Hunters disappeared into it. Avalanches swept down without warning, and streams flooded paths in thaw. The mountain was not neutral. It watched, it punished, it rewarded. That watchfulness gave the Namahage their natural home: figures descending from the slopes into the lights of the village below.

To an outsider, these forces might look like scenery. To the people of Oga, they were neighbors, close, capricious, and in need of acknowledgment. Ritual was how that acknowledgment was made. You bowed to the shrine not because you thought a painted board required it, but because the sea behind that shrine demanded respect. You offered grain at the harvest not only to thank the gods but to remind your children that abundance was never permanent. Out of this logic, the Namahage were inevitable.

Even before the name, before the masks, the pattern was set. Villagers knew that fear could be used as instruction. They told children that the mountain would take them if they wandered, that the sea would drag them if they were careless, that spirits would notice laziness and punish it. These were not idle threats. They were warnings sharpened by centuries of observation. A boy who disobeyed and strayed too far might be found frozen in a drift. A fisherman who delayed mending his nets might lose his catch and starve his family. Nature itself was the first disciplinarian. The Namahage only gave it a face.

When you imagine the demons pounding on doors, shouting questions into homes, you should not see them as intrusions from myth but as condensations of the landscape's authority. Their straw coats are fields carried inside. Their masks are mountains carved into wood. Their voices are the sea made audible in human breath. They do not belong only to folklore; they belong to the environment that demanded vigilance and gave punishment.

This foreshadowing matters because it explains why Oga's ritual never softened into entertainment. The Namahage are not imported villains or borrowed gods. They are indigenous to the peninsula's conditions. Their ferocity matches the ferocity of the weather. Their timing, at the turn of the year, matches the rhythm of survival: winter's hardest stretch still to come, households needing a reminder to keep discipline.

Other regions of Japan also developed rituals of visitation, but many lost their bite. Some became polite ceremonies, others faded as urban life softened their edges. In Oga, the land itself prevented softening. The snow did not relent. The sea did not forgive. As long as those forces remained, the figures that embodied them could not be declawed. The Namahage endured because the land that created them endured.

In this way, the geography of Oga is not backdrop but origin story. The fist of land thrust into the sea, the storms that erase boundaries, the forests that brood in silence, all of these are prefaces to the knock at the door. To write about the Namahage without writing about Oga would be to tell only half the story. The demons are not masks worn by men; they are the peninsula itself stepping briefly into human form.

When villagers hear the pounding at their threshold on New Year's Eve, they are hearing more than neighbors in disguise. They are hearing the sea's insistence that no one can afford to be idle, the snow's warning that unpreparedness is fatal, the mountain's reminder that humans live only at its pleasure. The Namahage arrive not as actors but as envoys of these larger truths.

This is why the ritual feels inevitable. Even if no one had carved masks or woven straw coats, Oga would still have found a way to summon figures of fear and instruction. In a land where survival requires effort, the imagination naturally produces visitors who enforce that effort. The Namahage are simply the form that inevitability took.

And so the stage is set. The land has foreshadowed the ritual, the people have prepared the roles, and the year turns toward its hardest season. The next step is to give the visitors names, shapes, and voices. From gods to demons, from mountain spirits to straw-clad neighbors, the Namahage emerge from the landscape into the household. That story begins in the next chapter.

CHAPTER 3: ORIGINS AND ETYMOLOGY

Section 1: Earliest Records & Cultural Context

When you first hear the Namahage pounding at the door, it feels like an eruption from nowhere. But rituals never arrive out of emptiness. They are shaped by the long traffic of stories, symbols, and beliefs that pass between cultures over centuries. To trace the Namahage back to its beginnings, you have to imagine the Oga Peninsula not only as an isolated landscape of snow and sea, but as a shoreline open to currents of influence drifting across East Asia.

Japan has always absorbed, reworked, and localized outside ideas. Buddhism arrived from India by way of China and Korea. Written script came with Chinese characters, which reshaped Japan's oral traditions into recorded chronicles. Festivals, deities, and demons all traveled these same routes. What began as Indian rakshasas, fierce spirits who punish the unrighteous, became Chinese oni, horned ogres feared as bringers of calamity. In Japan, those oni arrived not only as invaders in stories but as moral symbols, embodiments of human weakness or vice. The Namahage, though rooted in Oga's soil, carry this genealogy in their horns and teeth.

References to malevolent beings appear in the eighth-century chronicles Kojiki and Nihon Shoki, though not yet in the familiar horned form. Across the Heian and medieval periods the oni comes into focus in setsuwa collections, picture scrolls, and temple tales, a figure that can devastate, tempt, or test. As the image moves from distant myth to repeatable story, it enters folktales, shrine calendars, and moral lessons. By the time early modern villages wrote down their customs, "oni" could mean an enemy to be repelled or a visitor who checks conduct. That shift, from monster to examiner, made the figure available to ritual.

Oga's Namahage are not directly mentioned in those ancient chronicles, but their outlines emerge in regional records centuries later. Local documents from the Edo period describe young men dressing as demons and visiting homes at New Year's. These accounts stress two elements that endure to this day: the accusations of laziness, and the demands for promises of improvement. That these details appear in writing by the seventeenth and eighteenth centuries suggests the practice was already old, already codified, already accepted as more than mere mischief.

But to stop at Edo records would be to miss the deeper context. The practice of ritual visitation, strangers entering homes, frightening children, demanding better behavior, is not unique to Oga. It belongs to a much wider family of customs spread across Japan and beyond. The *toshigami* of Shinto, deities of the New Year, were believed to visit households at the year's turn, bringing fortune or misfortune depending on how they were received. Farmers laid out offerings for them, hoping to secure good harvests. In some regions, villagers disguised themselves as these gods, carrying the presence of renewal door to door. The Namahage echo this logic: a figure from outside enters to set the house in order.

At the same time, the Namahage carry traces of older, harsher spirits. In ancient Japan, demons were not only imported ideas but local fears. Mountain deities punished trespass, river spirits drowned the careless, storms were read as the wrath of unseen beings. These spirits were not abstract symbols but forces that explained sudden disaster. A ritual that embodied such figures inside the household was a way of acknowledging their power while also domesticating it, making it part of the community's cycle rather than a random strike from outside.

The blending of these traditions, Shinto gods of renewal, Buddhist-Chinese oni of punishment, local spirits of land and sea, produced the form we now recognize. A mask with horns, a voice demanding obedience, a timing tied to New Year's Eve when renewal was most urgent. What we call "Namahage" is not the invention of a single moment but the condensation of centuries of cultural layering.

Historical context matters here too. In premodern Japan, discipline was not optional. Survival depended on work done at the right time, by the right hands, in the right rhythm. Idleness threatened the entire household, even the village. Parents needed tools to impress this lesson on their children, and ritual provided one of the strongest. A terrifying visitor was more memorable than a lecture. A shouted question carried more weight than a polite reminder. The Namahage gave shape to what parents already knew: that fear, carefully staged, could instruct where reason alone might fail.

We must also remember how religion and daily life intertwined. To modern eyes, rituals are often seen as separate from "ordinary" tasks. But in Edo-period Oga, there was no such separation. The same men who fished or farmed by day could don straw coats by night and embody spirits. The same women who prepared rice for the family would set aside offerings for gods. To them, the Namahage were not performance but continuity, part of the same cycle that governed planting, harvesting, and praying for safety at sea.

Some scholars caution against overemphasizing foreign influence. They argue that Oga's demons are fundamentally local, born from the peninsula's particular conditions rather than imported ideas. This is a fair point. But the truth is not either-or.

The Namahage are both: local expressions of global symbols. Horned demons punishing idleness could be found in Chinese parables, in Buddhist temple carvings, in Indian sutras. Oga did not invent horns or shouting. What it invented was the specific ritual of pounding on doors, accusing children, and demanding promises on New Year's Eve. That synthesis is uniquely Oga's.

When villagers in the seventeenth century wrote down the practice, they were preserving something already old. When we hear the pounding today, we are hearing echoes that stretch back far beyond any surviving document. We cannot know the exact moment when a man first carved a mask and pulled straw across his shoulders. But we can say that the conditions for it existed centuries before: a land of hardship, a culture familiar with demons and gods of punishment, a need for discipline enforced by ritual. Out of this matrix, the Namahage emerged, not as folklore for display, but as living necessity.

What makes the Namahage remarkable is not that they resemble demons elsewhere, but that they survived. Many regions once had similar customs, figures who visited at the year's turn, who frightened children into better behavior. Most faded under the weight of modernization, urbanization, or simple disuse. Oga's endured. Its persistence suggests that the Namahage were not just decoration but indispensable. They spoke directly to the peninsula's reality, and so they were kept alive.

By the time outsiders took note, the ritual was already deeply woven into Oga's identity. It was not "invented tradition" in the sense of something staged for tourists or officials. It was lived, repeated, and handed down. The earliest records are only shadows of what had already been long practiced. To understand those shadows, we must look beyond the documents and into the cultural streams that fed them.

The Namahage's horns, straw, and roar are not arbitrary. Buddhism carried Indian rakshasa imagery into East Asia as luocha (羅刹), which in Japan became rasetsu (羅刹). Alongside this imported demonology, Japan's own category of oni, shaped by Chinese texts and local belief, absorbed horned, punitive traits. At the same time, Shinto's New Year visitors (Raiho-shin) and local spirits of snow and sea anchored the rite in place. All these currents met on the peninsula and poured into the mask. What steps across the threshold on New Year's Eve is not a novelty but a vessel for centuries of belief, shaped by the land and refined by necessity.

The pounding on the door may feel sudden. But when you hear it, you are listening to something ancient, a ritual voice that has been traveling for a thousand years before arriving in that moment at your threshold.

Section 2: Etymology of Namahage

Names are never just labels. They are arguments, compressed into a few syllables. To understand the Namahage, it is not enough to look at their horns, masks, or rituals, you have to weigh the name itself, because the name explains what the figure is meant to do.

Namahage is often glossed with the characters 生剥—"raw/peel"—which point directly to its meaning. In ordinary writing it appears in katakana (ナマハゲ). The usual etymology links namomi, the hearth blisters from lingering by the fire, and hagi (剥ぎ, "peeling"), from hagu (剥ぐ, "to peel"). Over time, namomi-hagi contracted to namahage.

This etymology gives the figure its job description: namomi o hagu—"peel off the fire blisters"—turns laziness into a surface to be scraped away. The name defines the visitor's role more than its shape.

This linguistic root is not incidental. It reveals how intimately the ritual was tied to everyday life. In Oga, laziness was not a vague moral failing; it was a visible, physical condition. The hearth was both survival and temptation. You needed it to live, but to lean on it too long was a form of weakness. Parents could point to the welts on a child's skin and say, "The Namahage will come for you." The name carried with it the moral weight of both necessity and shame.

Etymology often conceals as much as it reveals. Some folklorists argue that the connection to fire blisters may not be the original meaning but a later rationalization. It is possible that *nama* once meant "raw" or "unboiled" in the sense of "unrefined," while *hage* might derive from *hagu* (to strip away) in a more general sense. In this reading, the Namahage are not only punishing children for sitting by the fire, but stripping away the "raw" qualities of the human heart, idleness, deceit, disobedience. The ritual becomes purification, scraping off what is unfit so that the community can enter the new year cleansed.

Whichever reading you favor, the emphasis is the same: the Namahage are not demons for their own sake, but for the sake of discipline. Their name encodes the function of the ritual. The mask terrifies, but the word instructs. You are meant to know from the sound of it what the figure demands.

Language has its own authority in Japan, where the written character is as revered as the spoken word. In shrines, priests inscribe talismans with brush and ink, believing that the written form itself carries power. The word *Namahage*, written in bold strokes, was not just description but invocation. To say the name aloud was to call forth the act of stripping away laziness. Children did not need an academic explanation; they understood in their bodies what the word meant. They had seen their own skin blister from fire. They knew what it felt like to have weakness exposed.

The etymology also reflects the broader cultural structure of Japanese morality, where shame plays a central role. The *namomi* blister is both a private mark and a public sign. Everyone can see it. To have it noticed is to be embarrassed, to have your laziness made visible. The Namahage, then, are the ritual embodiment of this principle: they take what is hidden. idleness, deceit, disobedience, and drag it into the open, shouting it in front of family and neighbors. They are shame given form. The very name makes this explicit.

Another layer of meaning comes from the rhythm of the word itself. *Namahage* is four heavy syllables, each one sharp at the back of the mouth. In the dialect of Akita, it is spoken with a guttural edge, almost spat rather than said. The sound itself has a rasp, as if the name were already the scrape of straw against wood, the peel of skin from blister. This auditory quality reinforces the ritual's authority. A child does not forget the way the syllables crash into the air. The word itself is half a blow.

It is striking that the etymology focuses not on the mask, the horns, or the costume, but on idleness. In other cultures, demons are named for their appearance or their mythic roles: "devourer," "ogre," "beast." In Oga, the demon is named for the act of correction it performs. The name says less about what the Namahage are and more about what they do. They peel away. They strip off. They expose. The name is function, not form.

This linguistic orientation reinforces the view that the Namahage are not supernatural intruders but social tools. They are not named like gods, with lofty titles, but like workers with a task. Their job is clear in the word: remove laziness, peel off weakness. That bluntness is part of their power.

Some scholars note that in dialect, variations of the name existed: *Namomi-hagi* or *Namahage-sama*, with the suffix "-sama" conferring honor. These variations remind us that the figure's status could slide between fearsome and sacred. To call them *sama* was to acknowledge them as more than village youths in costume; it was to treat them as divine visitors. The same word, stretched in meaning, could balance demon and deity.

The word also connects Oga's custom to a larger pattern of Japanese ritual naming. Many traditional festivals feature figures whose names directly describe their roles. In some regions, "blessing-strikers" or "fortune-bringers" visit households, their names telling you exactly what they carry. The Namahage fit neatly into this pattern. They are "blister-peelers," and so they peel away vice.

To modern ears, the name might sound quaint, even a little grotesque. But in the context of Oga's winters, it was perfectly clear. When the door shook and the voice thundered "Are there any lazy children here?" the name itself explained why the demons had come. They were not random terrors. They were the ones who peel away what is soft, what is idle, what is unfit for survival.

If Section 1 showed us the Namahage as a synthesis of gods, demons, and local spirits, the etymology brings us closer to their lived meaning. The name is the bridge between myth and household. It translates cosmic discipline into the language of blisters and hearths. It anchors the ritual in the body, in the skin itself.

What is in a name? For the Namahage, everything. The horns could change shape, the masks could differ by village, but the word remained the same. It carried the memory of winters, the sting of shame, the scrape of correction. To say *Namahage* is to say: discipline has entered the room.

Section 3: Competing Origin Stories

If the Namahage's name reveals their purpose, their stories reveal their possibilities. In Oga, as in much of rural Japan, myth is not fixed. It is retold, adapted, contradicted, and re-shaped according to what a community needs to believe. Ask three elders where the Namahage came from, and you may hear three different stories, none of them mutually exclusive. The figures at the door are protean, shifting between gods, demons, and ancestors, depending on the frame of the tale.

The first origin begins with five ogres arriving from across the Sea of Japan and coming ashore on the Oga Peninsula. They raid granaries and seize young women. The villagers set a wager before witnesses: if the ogres can build a flight of stone steps up Mount Shinzan before the first rooster crows, the land and its people will be theirs; if they fail, they must depart forever. The ogres agree and work through the winter night, hauling boulders into rough courses toward the summit. In the hour before dawn, a villager mimics a rooster. Taking the cry for morning, the ogres drop their stones and flee. Locals still point to broken runs of steps—"999" in some tellings—on the approach to Goshadō, the five-hall complex of Akagami Shrine, as material trace of the failed claim.

At surface level the story functions as an etiological map. It ties visible stonework on Shinzan and the Goshadō precincts to a single, memorable night, turning landscape into proof a listener can visit. The motif is old and portable: superhuman construction that must finish "in one night," and a last-minute failure that preserves local sovereignty. Oga's version is unusually specific about place names and stair counts, which likely helped its endurance.

The "five" matters because it is native to the tale's best-known Oga variant, not because we need it to carry a theory. In one strand the entourage originates with Emperor Wu of Han and his *five* bats that transform into *five* oni; in others the emperor sends five ogres outright. Either way, the number is in the local record, and the Goshadō complex itself is a row of five halls. That resonance with East Asian sets of five, directions when the center is counted, Five Phases, "five grains"—is suggestive, but there is no hard evidence the story was composed to encode those systems.

The contest on the mountain is a test of strength types. The ogres wield force; the villagers wield timing and shared signal. The hinge is a rooster's voice, which in Japan marks daybreak ritually as well as naturally. In Shinto contexts roosters are associated with awakening the sun goddess and the return of order at dawn; a cockcrow is, in effect, a cue for nocturnal beings to withdraw. The villagers exploit that logic early and win without blood.

Placed against Oga's maritime setting, the legend reads as social memory: Sea of Japan operated as corridor more often than moat. Traders, monks, drifters, and pirates connected Korea, China, and the Tōhoku coast. A coastal community accustomed to sudden landfalls would remember demands made by strangers and the need for concerted, lawful responses. The tale compresses those realities into a single night and turns anxiety into a rehearsable answer.

Two details bind the story to practice. First, the "999/1000 steps" are a monument aborted at the threshold of sovereignty; halting their completion prevents the ogres from naturalizing their claim. Second, the residue matters more than the departure: stones on the slope and a calendared knock at the door. In midwinter, masked visitors cross household thresholds to admonish idleness and demand promises, a domesticated echo of the seaborne intruders who once demanded tribute. The figures still arrive from "outside," but they now serve the village's governance rather than threaten it.

Finally, the bargain structure clarifies why the tale remains legible to children and useful to adults. It is simple enough to remember, wager, deadline, trick, retreat, and sufficiently anchored in place that a guide can show its "evidence." When the Namahage pound doors on Ōmisoka, they invert the old asymmetry: the visiting power tests the house, departs on schedule, and leaves order behind. The mountain keeps its scattered stones; the village keeps a story for meeting whatever may arrive across the water next.

Another origin locates the Namahage within Japan's New Year theology. In this reading they are not ogres but visiting Toshigami, deities who come at the year's turn to renew fields and families. Oshōgatsu, the New Year, was framed as a welcome for these gods. Households cleansed rooms, settled debts, and marked thresholds so the divine could cross them. The expectation was concrete. Families placed kadomatsu (pine and bamboo gate ornaments) at entrances, hung shimenawa (sacred straw ropes) to mark a purified boundary, and set out kagami mochi (stacked rice cakes) as food for the visiting presence. Much of today's holiday customs, including hatsumōde (the first shrine visit), rests on that premise of visitation rather than abstract celebration.

Seen from that angle, the Namahage are one local form of a wider class of visiting beings, the raiho-shin. These are presences that arrive from outside ordinary space on calendrical nights, test the household, accept offerings, and depart so that normal time can resume. Oga's New Year timing fits that logic exactly. The figures appear on the final night of the year, cross the sill, speak as if from beyond the village, and then withdraw. The point is not spectacle. It is renewal that depends on a guest being properly received.

The parallels run through the entire sequence of the visit. Toshigami are expected once a year and only once. Namahage arrive on that same fixed night. Toshigami purify and bless. Namahage purge idleness and promise protection from misfortune in the coming cycle. Toshigami are fed. Namahage accept rice cakes, sake, and prepared dishes that mirror the offerings set for the gods. Toshigami depart so that everyday life can begin cleanly. Namahage leave on schedule and do not linger past midnight. The script is consistent with a divine call and response rather than mere theatrics.

The material signs also line up. Straw in Oga is not only a fiber. It is the same substance as the ropes that mark sacred space. When a figure wrapped in straw crosses a threshold hung with straw, the household is watching two registers of the same idea. A dangerous, untamed power from mountain and field is being admitted and contained for the sake of fertility and safety. The mask reads as ferocity to a child. To an adult in this frame it reads as the wild, made useful.

Offerings make the continuity visible. In the Toshigami schema, food is not a payoff. It is reciprocity. The family hosts a powerful guest and receives protection in return. Oga preserves that exchange. Households prepare sake and foods that echo **osechi** (New Year dishes) and present them to the figures, who accept and move on. What looks like appeasement from outside sits squarely within a sacred economy that is older than the mask. People give. The visitor blesses. The year can start.

Shrine practice in Oga supports the same interpretation. The Namahage Sedo Festival is staged on shrine grounds and folds the house-to-house visitation into a fire rite that is explicitly

Shinto. Priests oversee offerings. The figures move among worshippers as divine guests rather than as anonymous youths. When they finally withdraw they are said to return to the deep mountain where the god resides. The language matches the New Year theology in which a presence comes near and then recedes until the next hinge of the calendar.

Taking the Toshigami frame seriously does not require erasing other memories of origin. It clarifies why the ritual belongs to New Year rather than any other season and why its actions look the way they do. The door must be prepared. The guest must be honored. The household must answer aloud that it will keep the rules that keep life going. The departure must be guaranteed so that ordinary time can start clean. Within that order, fear has a purpose and a limit.

As an origin theory, this account is simple and sufficient. Rural Japan already had a language for deities who visit at the year's turn and a set of household practices designed for that welcome. Oga's Namahage fit those expectations point by point. What appears to be a night of demons resolves, under this light, into the return of the year gods by another name.

A third origin theory places the Namahage in the mountains themselves. In Oga they are remembered as yama no kami, "mountain gods," who descend each winter to inspect conduct and renew order. Local accounts make the link plain. Oga is read as a mountain that rises out of the sea, and a protective god is said to dwell there. In this view the Namahage act as that god's messengers. Some tellings add that the figures once appeared at Koshogatsu, the first full moon of the year, and that today's Sedo rites at Shinzan Shrine reenact the same pattern. The figures descend from the mountain, move among households and worshippers, accept what is offered, and then return to the mountain so ordinary time can begin clean.

This theology fits the place. Oga's ridges are steep and snowbound. The growing season is short. Storms and landslides can cut a hamlet from the coast without warning. The same slopes that give timber, water, and safe vantage can also take lives. In regions like this, mountain deities are invoked as guardians who bless and punish. Their authority is seasonal. They are imagined to dwell high and then to come down at calendrical thresholds when people most need favor.

Mountain cults across rural Japan follow a simple logic. Boundaries are marked in advance so the crossing is safe. Taboos keep the exchange clean. Offerings of rice, sake, and produce acknowledge that human work depends on permission from the heights. The visitation functions as inspection as much as blessing. The deity verifies diligence and restraint, the two habits that keep a settlement in balance with its terrain.

Read against that pattern, the Namahage fit cleanly. Their timing is winter, just before the new year's work begins. Their direction is from mountain to household and back again. Their function is to warn against idleness and to demand promises that merit next year's bounty. A family prepares the sill. The figures enter as if from beyond the village. They speak in the voice of the land that sustains the people. They accept what is offered and then withdraw so that normal time can resume.

Material details support the link. Straw is not only a covering for the body. It is the same substance used to mark purified space in shrine practice, a sign that raw power from field and mountain is being admitted and contained. Fire rites at the foot of the slope, including the Sedo fire that anchors the festival at Shinzan, dramatize the passage between wild ground and settled ground. Food and sake given to the visitors mirror agrarian exchanges with a tutelary power. People give from the harvest they have and ask permission to seek another.

Later interpreters have also seen in the Namahage echoes of *yamabushi*, ascetics of the Shugendo tradition who likewise emerged from mountain fastnesses to admonish villagers. The resemblance in dress and bearing is striking, yet this belongs to a different layer of religious history than the older mountain-god belief. The proximity is instructive without being the same. It helps explain why a winter visitor from the heights can be heard both as divine command and as human admonition.

Taken together, the geography, the shrine rites, and the house-to-house script make the mountain-gods theory a credible beginning. The ritual belongs to the season when the mountain is closest. A power from outside the household enters, tests, accepts, and departs. The village answers, and the year can start.

Asking which origin is "correct" mistakes how living ritual works. Practices like the Namahage do not spring from a single source. They accumulate. A community keeps more than one explanation in play because each speaks to a different need. In Oga, the figures can be foreigners from the sea, visiting New Year deities, or mountain gods. None cancels the others. Each supplies a frame for the same rite.

What binds the frames is function. The constants are clear. A calendared night at the year's hinge. A visitor from outside ordinary space. A threshold crossed. Questions that test diligence and order. Offerings given and accepted. A guaranteed departure so normal time can resume. The stories explain why the visitor has authority. The script shows what that authority does.

The mix is also practical. When fear of outsiders is salient, the sea tale explains the knock at the door. When New Year theology is foregrounded, Toshigami logic makes the visit purification rather than menace. When the land sets the terms of survival, the mountain gods give the figures a local voice. As conditions shift, the preferred explanation shifts with them while the rite remains intact.

This plurality helps the custom endure. A single story can age badly. A set of stories lets meaning move without altering the work the ritual performs. Children still tremble. Parents still answer for the household. The village still rehearses a bargain with powers larger than itself.

Section 4: Transition to Ritual

Legends explain beginnings, but rituals explain survival. Stories of foreign ogres or mountain gods give the Namahage grandeur, but codifying their visits into a yearly custom gave them endurance. Without ritual, the Namahage might have remained half-remembered tales tied to boulders on a hillside or to the whisper of deities in winter storms. With ritual, they became unavoidable: knocks at every door, shouts in every household, promises extracted from every child. The transition from myth to custom turned them from folklore into lived reality.

In many parts of Japan the New Year was the time when gods were believed to descend. Toshigami brought renewal, cleansing households for the cycle ahead. On Oga, this cosmology met harsher local needs: vigilance against idleness, fear of winter's grip, the demand for discipline that survival required. Prayer honored the divine guest, but a visible, audible visit could enforce norms. At some point the two threads met. A sacred visitation took embodied form in horned figures whose authority was understood rather than explained.

The exact moment of change cannot be pinned down. The written record is sparse, and like much of rural tradition the Namahage ceremony passed by word of mouth, shaped more by repetition than by documents. By the Edo period (seventeenth to nineteenth centuries), regional accounts describe masked visitors on New Year's Eve who berated children and accepted sake. The pattern appears already standardized. The visit was annual, the route was comprehensive, households expected it, and participation was not optional.

This shift matters. When a story becomes a ritual, it gains authority over memory. A myth can fade. A repeated act writes itself into bodies and rooms. Parents prepared, children dreaded, neighbors watched. Each year's visit renewed the last. What may have begun as a spontaneous impersonation of a visiting power became a calendar-bound obligation. The gods were not only remembered, they were enacted.

The choice of date is no accident. December 31 is Ōmisoka, the great eve, the hinge between the old year and the new. It was, and remains, one of Japan's most charged nights. On this threshold impurities are swept away, debts are repaid, and households are made clean to welcome the toshigami. On Oga, the Namahage took place within that liminal space. They did not wait for the new year to arrive gently. They announced it with fists on wood and voices raised against laziness. Fixed to this night, their accusations worked as purification. The year did not turn until households had faced them and promised reform.

Preparation matched the seriousness of the visit. Houses were put in order, hearths were tended, offerings were set aside, and children were warned to answer plainly. The sequence itself became legible to everyone present. A loud entry. A round of accusations. A negotiation in which the head of household answered and offered. An instruction for the year ahead. A withdrawal that signaled the house had passed its test.

The annual rhythm set the Namahage apart from other festivities. Dances could be postponed, fairs skipped. The Namahage were not optional. They were coming, and everyone knew it. Obligation gave the rite its weight. Routes were predictable, house to house, without omission. Variation by hamlet was tolerated in costume and speech, but the core script held.

Roles hardened as the custom matured. By long convention, younger men of the village, often unmarried or apprenticed, donned masks and straw coats. Their energy suited the task. They could stomp, shout, and terrify without flagging. On the surface this made the figures convincingly otherworldly. Beneath the surface it served as a rite of passage. For a night a farmer's son could roar at his elders, demand promises of his neighbors and be treated as a force of authority.

Such inversion is a common engine of ritual. The young dominated the old, the childless admonished parents, the masked outshouted the unmasked. Because the inversion was bounded by tradition, it strengthened rather than threatened the social fabric. The next day roles reverted. The men returned to fields and boats with the memory of power and the knowledge of responsibility.

Universality was another defining feature. The Namahage visited every home. The mayor's children trembled no less than the fisherman's. Universality created fairness and inevitability. No child could claim exemption. No parent could sidestep accountability. It also made the ordeal bearable. Shame isolates when it singles out a few. When everyone endures it together, shame becomes communal and less corrosive. Over time this universality cemented the ritual's authority. The visit became a shared rhythm like planting or harvest. Refusal would have meant exclusion from the community itself.

This is how myths harden into institutions. What begins as the story of an ogre or a god becomes, through repetition, a social mechanism. By the time outside observers wrote about Oga in the early modern period, the figures were no longer just folklore. They were part of governance, one of the ways a community regulated itself. The fear they inspired was real, but it was contained by structure: accusation, negotiation, instruction, release.

Children perceived chaos. Adults saw order. The pounding on wood, the shouted questions, the sweep of straw across tatami, all followed a script. Improvisation was allowed. Randomness was not. The Namahage embodied terror, but the terror was rehearsed. That is what made it bearable, and therefore effective.

There is a paradox at the heart of the transition. By assigning roles and fixing dates, villagers risked stripping away divine unpredictability. A god is wild and unknowable. A ritual is scheduled and knowable. Did fixing the date weaken the Namahage? In practice, the opposite proved true. Predictability ensured survival. Gods can be forgotten. Myths can fade. Rituals that bind a community year after year persist. The Namahage's power moved from the realm of belief to the realm of practice. No one had to decide whether demons were real. They had to open the door on December 31 and face them.

That is the work of ritual. It takes what is fleeting, story and fear and divine presence, and gives it permanence through repetition. The Namahage may once have been mountain gods or foreign ogres. By the time they became obligatory visitors they were something more enduring: the embodiment of discipline enacted annually so that no one could forget.

CHAPTER 4: The Masks: Faces of Fear

Section 1: Craft and Material

The mask is the face of the ritual, but it is also the face of the craftsman who carved it. Every chisel mark, every groove, every asymmetry is the trace of a hand that shaped fear into wood. To speak of Namahage masks only as costumes misses their weight: they are living artifacts, built not just to frighten children but to carry a community's memory, and they do so because someone, usually someone in the village, gave weeks of labor to a single block of wood.

In Oga, mask-makers traditionally drew from what the peninsula offered. Japanese cedar (sugi) and paulownia (kiri) were the workhorses, cedar abundant and forgiving under the chisel, paulownia light and easy to hollow for hours of wear. Some artisans also used cypress (hinoki), prized for its fine grain and clean edges, though less typical locally than cedar. Each wood brought its own weight and smell: cedar resinous and warm, paulownia pale and quick to take shape, hinoki taking pigment evenly and finishing to a quiet sheen. Choice began as practicality, what grew here and what a man could carry, before it became symbolism.

The selection was never arbitrary. A block chosen for a Namahage mask was not just lumber but potential spirit. Older carvers spoke of listening to the wood, running hands along the grain, tapping with knuckles for resonance, judging the way the piece wanted to be cut. A log could sit for months seasoning, leaning against the wall of a shed until its moisture settled. Cutting too green meant warping later, a crack across the brow, a fissure down a horn. Patience, even before the first strike of the chisel, was part of the craft.

There was lore, too. Wood taken in winter was said to be denser, its sap withdrawn, its fibers tight with the season's discipline. A mask carved from winter wood carried that discipline into its face. Some carvers insisted that cedar felled at dawn had a straighter grain than cedar cut at dusk. Whether this was botany or superstition mattered little, the act of choosing lent reverence to the material.

The tools of a mask-maker are deceptively simple: chisels, mallets, knives, scrapers. Yet simplicity hides depth. A chisel must be sharpened to a hair's edge, and sharpened again between strokes if the cut grows dull. A mallet strike too heavy will shear away more than intended; too light, and the cut will chatter, leaving a scar where smoothness was needed. The mask is the sum of thousands of such decisions, each one irreversible.

Older artisans likened the relationship to that between swordsmith and hammer. Just as the hammer's fall must be attuned to the steel's heat, so the chisel's bite must be attuned to the grain's direction. To gouge against the grain is to fight the wood and invite splintering. To cut with it is to release form with almost no resistance, as if the mask were already waiting inside.

Many tools were inherited, their wooden handles polished black by generations of hands. Some carried nicks and stains from previous works, reminders that the tool was not just steel but lineage. To sharpen was to honor both ancestors and descendants. A dull chisel was not just inefficient; it was disrespectful.

The first stage was always the block-out: roughing the general shape of the mask from the raw plank or log. Here the craftsman worked in bold strokes, chopping planes for forehead, cheekbones, jaw. There was little detail, only geometry. Yet even this early stage demanded vision. A line cut too deep across the brow might make the forehead too shallow; a jawline taken in haste might leave no space for teeth. The face's power lies in its proportions, and those had to be envisioned while the block still looked like little more than firewood.

Hollowing came next. A mask cannot be dead weight; it has to sit on a man's face and move with his voice. Carvers gouged from the back, scooping out curls of wood until the mask was both light and resonant. The first moment the hollowing broke through to thinness was said to be the moment the mask took breath. A solid block is inert. A hollow form echoes. The echo makes the roar louder, the presence larger. Many artisans paused at this moment, tapping the mask's back and listening to its new voice.

Only then did the features emerge. Eyes were carved as ovals or narrow slits, cut wide enough for vision yet shaped to glare under lamplight. Teeth were often stylized into sharp fangs, sometimes exaggerated for effect but always ordered enough to be read as a mouth that could bite or roar. A mouth might be carved open to an unnatural width, frozen mid-shout, emphasizing sound over speech. Horns were added last, pegged separately into the crown, their forms varying from long ox-like curves to shorter, brutish stubs.

Color finished the transformation. Red masks seemed to blaze, their heat suggesting fury or punishment. Blue masks carried a colder edge, echoing the winter wind outside the door or a severity that chilled as much as it threatened. While less common, green masks sometimes appeared. Paint was thick, applied in bold strokes, then sealed with lacquer to give the surface a hard shine. In dim lamplight, the gleam made the masks seem wet, as if sweating or breathing. Some carvers left the paint thin, the grain of the wood showing through like veins beneath skin.

The final touch was the strap, cord or cloth tied through drilled holes to fix the mask to a man's head. The strap was practical, but it was also symbolic. To put it on was to bind oneself to the role. Once tied, the man was no longer himself.

For centuries, mask-making was not a commercial craft but a communal duty. Certain families, often carpenters or shrine carvers, took on the responsibility of producing or repairing masks for their villages. Skills passed from father to son, uncle to nephew, master to apprentice. A boy might begin by sharpening tools, sweeping shavings, or painting underlayers. Only after years would he be allowed to carve eyes or mouths, the features that gave the mask life.

In Oga today, a few recognized artisans carry the tradition forward, producing masks both for ritual use and for display. Their workshops are half museum, half forge, walls lined with faces at every stage, some grimacing half-finished, others gleaming with fresh lacquer. Tourists may see them as souvenirs, but within the community, the masks retain their older weight. To buy a mask is to purchase an object. To make one for ritual use is to take part in continuity.

Some carvers describe a sense that the wood resists or guides their hand, as if the mask already existed inside the block and their task was only to reveal it. Superstition perhaps, but revealing of belief: that the mask is not inert wood but something that can answer back, something into which presence descends.

One of the striking features of Namahage masks is their boldness. Unlike the serene, polished surfaces of Noh masks, Namahage masks are carved to exaggerate: brows cut in deep furrows, mouths forced open in a permanent roar, fangs gleaming against painted skin. Their symmetry is intact, but their proportions are pushed beyond the human, into something larger and harsher. A face like this is not meant to charm, it is meant to confront.

Today, mass-produced masks are common and sold widely, yet many communities still value masks carved by local artisans for the December 31st ritual. The difference is not in whether one can frighten, any horned face in a dark doorway will make a child's heart stutter, but in what the mask carries. A hand-carved mask smells of cedar shavings and fresh lacquer, its grooves still bearing the touch of the knife. That intimacy matters. The mask is not distant or generic; it is rooted in the village, in the hands of neighbors, and that connection deepens the ritual's power.

The act of making a Namahage mask is not just technical but philosophical. The carver knows he is not creating a piece of art to be admired silently as a display. He is creating an instrument of transformation. In the hands of its wearer, the mask will terrify children, humble parents, and cleanse households. The stakes are high: carve too weakly, and the mask loses presence; carve too cleanly, and it becomes pretty rather than terrifying.

In this sense, mask-making shares kinship with other Japanese crafts that balance utility and spirit. A sword is not merely steel; it is a weapon shaped by ritual, polish, and reverence. A tea bowl is not merely clay; it is a vessel of hospitality, its imperfections cherished as *wabi-sabi*. The Namahage mask belongs in this lineage. It is not decorative. It is functional, but its function is fear.

To carve such an object requires humility. The craftsman knows he is channeling something larger than himself, ancestral presence, perhaps even divine authority. He knows the mask will outlast him, used year after year until it chips, cracks, and is replaced by another. His name may be forgotten, but the mask's voice will continue.

What makes the Namahage mask so enduring is precisely this: it is fear carved by hand. Each stroke of the chisel is intimate. Each groove is specific. The mask does not descend from heaven; it is built by a craftsman at his bench, bent over a block, listening to wood and shaping it until it stares back at him. And then that mask goes out into the snow, onto the face of another man, perhaps his own cousin or childhood friend, and frightens the children of the village.

That is the paradox and the genius: the fear is local, familiar, yet magnified. The child screams at a horned demon, not realizing he is screaming at the neighbor's son. The father bows to a snarling face, not acknowledging that he sharpened tools for that carver only last summer. The intimacy does not diminish the terror; it deepens it. Because if fear can come from your neighbor's hand, then fear can come from anywhere.

The mask, then, is not decoration. It is not even just ritual equipment. It is the face of accountability, shaped from local wood, carrying local breath, born of local hands. When the Namahage enter a home, they carry with them the labor of a craftsman who listened to grain and honored imperfection. The mask is terrifying precisely because it is human made, rather than divine. It is fear that comes from within the community, not from outside.

And so, each December, when the masks emerge from storage, smelling faintly of cedar and lacquer, they bring with them not just the terror of demons but the quiet authority of craft. The children see horns and teeth. The adults see chisels and labor. Both see fear, and both are right.

Section 2: Symbolism of Features

What gives the Namahage its power is not only the straw coat, the pounding fists, or the shouted questions. It is the face. The mask fixes the ritual in memory, the carved visage that children recall decades later with perfect clarity: the color, the horns, the eyes that did not blink. Without the mask, the ritual would be only a noisy intrusion. With it, the Namahage becomes something larger than the men inside.

The eyes of a Namahage mask are steady and fixed. Carved wide and round, or narrowed into slits, they radiate authority. In firelight or under the weak glow of an oil lamp, they catch and hold attention, glowing starkly against painted wood. Their fixity matters: they do not shift or soften, but stare forward without distraction, as though the gaze belonged not to a person but to judgment itself.

For children, those eyes become unbearable. The lack of motion offers no hint of humor or forgiveness. They look forward without pause, pinning the child in a gaze that seems both impartial and inescapable. Parents, too, feel the weight of that stare. It is the village's scrutiny made visible.

The mouth is usually open, cut wide so that the roar of the wearer can pour through it unimpeded. Inside are fangs, often the upper canines painted stark white against the darker cavity. The rest of the teeth are incidental, sometimes indicated with paint, sometimes not at all. What matters are the fangs, sharp and gleaming, proof that the being before you is a predator.

The symbolism is blunt but effective. Even the youngest child knows instinctively what fangs mean: threat, punishment, danger. When the Namahage shouts, the fangs amplify the message, turning words into something that feels physical. The mouth is not just a passage for sound but a weapon, and the lesson delivered through it is unforgettable.

From the brow rise the horns, always in pairs, always balanced. Their length and curve differ from mask to mask, some long and slightly bowed, others shorter and straighter, but they are never accidental. The horns place the Namahage squarely in the lineage of oni, the demons of Japanese folklore whose horned silhouettes are instantly recognized.

In the low interior of a farmhouse, the horns matter as much for their physical presence as their symbolism. They scrape against beams, brush paper lamps, enlarge the body of the demon until it feels too large for the room. The message is simple: this figure does not belong indoors. Its very shape disrupts the safe geometry of the house.

In their lacquered finish, red and blue dominate Namahage masks. Over time they have come to suggest different temperaments: red often read as fiery, punishing, restless; blue as colder, severe, carrying something of the winter outside the threshold. These are not rigid codes so much as impressions, reinforced year after year until the association feels natural. Other shades exist at the edges of the tradition. Some communities use green, linking the mask to the mountains and fertility or even envy. A few employ white, stark and spectral, unnerving in its purity. But the overwhelming impression in Oga is of red and blue. Generation after generation, children learn to recognize those hues as the signal that fear has entered the house.

Across the eyes stretch heavy brows, carved in deep ridges. The scowl is exaggerated, the shadow permanent. Beneath them, the forehead is broad, a solid plane of color that seems to press down upon the eyes like a lid. The expression cannot soften. It is locked into disapproval.

This permanence matters in a culture where expressions are usually restrained, emotions rarely made so public. The Namahage mask is the opposite of subtlety. It is judgment frozen in wood, displayed without nuance, brought into the home for all to see.

Beyond paint and carving, the mask's menace is often completed by its hair. Some masks bristle with straw or coarse fiber, sprouting from the chin or crown in unkempt tufts. These suggest beards or manes, but also reinforce the connection between the demon and the natural world. The material is rarely neat. It hangs wild, brushing against walls and children alike, a reminder that the Namahage comes not from the ordered interior but from the fields and mountains outside.

When straw grazes a child's cheek, the mask is no longer distant. It is tactile, intimate, a piece of the outside carried in to brush the skin. That detail lingers in memory as strongly as the roar itself.

Taken together, eyes, fangs, horns, brows, and hair form a deliberate vocabulary, a grammar of fear, consistent across generations and unforgettable to children and adults alike.

Although the Namahage are often spoken of as a single tradition, in practice no two masks are identical. Within the villages of Oga, artisans have always left small marks of individuality, a horn that tapers longer, a brow cut deeper, a mouth opened wider. These are not radical departures but accents within a shared vocabulary. For scholars, such differences are useful in tracing local lineages of craft. For villagers, they are subtler still.

Some masks were carved massive, with broad jaws and wide foreheads that overwhelmed the face of the wearer, making the Namahage appear larger than life even before the straw coat was added. Others were smaller and tighter to the face, relying less on scale and more on ferocity of expression. Scale was practical as much as aesthetic: heavy masks demanded stamina and suited younger men who could shoulder the weight, while smaller masks allowed quicker movement through the lanes, letting the demon strike and vanish. Such differences spoke less to strict regional rules than to the demands of the route, the stamina of the wearer, and the hand of the carver.

The carving of Namahage masks shows a noticeable range of individual approaches, sometimes even within the same village. Some masks are rough-hewn, with tool marks left visible in the wood; others are smoothed and sealed under layers of lacquer. Brows may be cut in deep furrows that cast permanent shadows, while in other hands the lines are softer, yielding a face closer to human but no less severe. The mouth, too, varies: some masks exaggerate fangs into tusks, while others rely on a wide-open maw to carry threat. Each detail reflects the hand of the artisan, so that even while the masks share a common theme, horns, fangs, glaring eyes, no two are identical.

These differences mattered in performance. A rough surface caught shadows, making the expression seem restless, as though the face itself twitched and shifted in the lamplight. A polished mask reflected the glow evenly, giving it a more severe, immovable authority, the kind of presence that seemed to judge rather than rage. Both methods carried intimidation, but in different registers: one alive with movement, the other imposing with stillness.

Minor variations in carving were not treated as mistakes. A deeper brow or heavier jaw did not weaken the mask but gave it distinction. In many cases, the carver was known to the community, often a craftsman from a family of carpenters or shrine workers, sometimes an apprentice entrusted with a feature for the first time. These traces of individuality were recognized, but they did not overshadow the ritual. What mattered was the pounding of boots, the shouts at the doorway, the repetition of tradition itself. The differences simply ensured that the Namahage never looked mass produced or duplicate in nature. Each mask carried the marks of real hands, and that familiarity, paradoxically, made the terror sharper.

Today, many older masks are preserved in local collections. At Shinzan, two institutions sit side by side. The Namahage Museum (Namahage-kan) displays rows of masks from across Oga, along with tools, photos, and recordings. Next door, the Oga Shinzan Folklore Museum (Shinzan Denshokan) stages the house-visit reenactment inside a traditional farmhouse. Seen together, they make the continuities and variations legible: the same horns and fangs, but each brow cut with a different weight, each mouth frozen at a different pitch of roar.

For the villagers, though, these masks were never primarily objects of art. They were tools, vessels meant to be worn, sweated into, and shouted through. A displayed mask is a reminder of the ritual, but a mask fitted to a face and carried into a farmhouse is the ritual itself. Preservation may serve museums and scholars, but carving serves the community, not to archive, but to continue.

For children, even the smallest change could feel striking. The pounding of boots and the shouts at the doorway might follow the same script year after year, but the face that leaned through the threshold was never quite the one they remembered. That difference preserved immediacy. It reminded families that the Namahage was not a relic or a reproduction but something still made, still alive in the village.

The masks of Oga are therefore not one mask but many. Each face reflects both the shared essence of the Namahage and the individuality of the carver. To outsiders the variations may seem minor, but to those within the peninsula they are marks of identity. This is the paradox of the Namahage: a single tradition that gains strength through multiplicity. The children who tremble before the mask are not only confronting a demon. They are confronting the face of their own community, sharpened into wood, carried forward by the hands of neighbors. The terror is communal, but so is the pride.

Section 3: Masks in Other Cultures

The Namahage mask, though rooted in northern Japan, speaks in a language that is nearly universal. Across cultures, ritual masks follow the same logic: symmetry for authority, exaggeration for fear, bright color for impact.

In Africa, initiation masks stare with round eyes and open mouths, teaching obedience through spectacle. In Oceania, ancestor masks enlarge features beyond human scale, transforming a villager into something ancestral and terrifying. European winter festivals also employ horned and fanged masks, designed to terrify children into proper conduct.

The parallels are not coincidence. Humans across the world have recognized the same truth: that fear, when embodied in wood and paint, can discipline in ways reason alone often cannot. The Namahage mask is Japan's iteration of this shared human instinct.

What endures in the Namahage mask is its clarity. There is no confusion about what the face represents. It does not flirt, cajole, or jest. It scowls, it roars, it threatens. And yet it does so within strict boundaries: the same faces appear each year, the same colors, the same horns, the same fangs.

This repetition makes the mask more than decoration. It becomes an icon, inseparable from the ritual itself. When villagers recall their childhoods, they rarely describe the straw coat or even the voices first. They remember the mask, the way it filled the doorway, the way its eyes would not look away, the way its color seemed alive in the firelight.

For the child, that memory is terror. For the adult, it is discipline recalled. For the community, it is the survival of tradition. A mask, after all, is more than wood and paint. It is the face of the collective will, preserved in a form that can be worn and enacted, year after year.

Section 4: The Mask as Archetype

Every Namahage mask, no matter how locally distinct, speaks to something larger than a village ritual. It belongs to a category of human expression that stretches across centuries and continents: the mask as archetype. To see the carved face at the threshold is to encounter not only a demon of Oga but the idea of fear itself, shaped into wood and painted into permanence.

The word "archetype" carries weight because it suggests patterns that recur in human imagination, the forms that human beings seem to rediscover again and again. Carl Jung described archetypes as inhabitants of the collective unconscious, surfacing in dreams, myths, and rituals. Whether or not one accepts Jung's theory in full, the evidence of repetition is undeniable. The horned face that terrifies a child in Akita resembles the horned faces carved into Alpine masks in Austria, in the Mamuthones of Sardinia, in the Kukeri of Bulgaria. The gaping mouth of the Namahage recalls the grotesque gargoyles that leer from the heights of European cathedrals, or the open-jawed guardian statues that line the gates of Buddhist temples. Across the world, people have devised masks that strip away individuality and replace it with something larger, something that insists on absolute presence.

One of the most immediate lessons of the Namahage mask is that authority does not come from personality. The man inside disappears. His features are erased. What remains is a constructed face that owes nothing to his identity. To the child at the doorway, it does not matter who is wearing the mask. It matters only that the mask has appeared, that a face has emerged which is not negotiable and not familiar.

This concealment is what grants the Namahage its authority. Words shouted from behind the carved mouth no longer sound like the voice of a neighbor or cousin. They sound like pronouncements from outside the family, outside the village, outside the human scale. Authority is created not by wealth, not by lineage, but by anonymity. The mask strips the wearer of himself and makes him a vessel for the ritual, amplifying his words into something communal and archetypal.

The effect is profound. A young man who could never scold an elder in daily life suddenly shouts commands with impunity. Children who know the gait and voice of their uncle cannot recognize him once the mask covers his face. Facelessness is not absence but transformation: it is what allows the community to hear judgment without resenting the judge, to feel terror without blaming the person. Authority is constructed precisely because the man has been erased.

The Namahage mask draws its strength from exaggeration. Eyes are rounder than human eyes, mouths wider, brows heavier. The features push beyond proportion, into the territory where recognition blurs into fear. This principle is found in masks across cultures: exaggeration seizes attention, shocks the senses, and denies the comfort of familiarity.

Modern psychology's "uncanny valley" offers a useful analogy here: forms that are recognizably human yet not quite human can unsettle, especially when they move in ways that are almost, but not exactly, lifelike. The Namahage mask is stylized rather than naturalistic, but its abrupt lunges, sudden freezes, and held stares push the encounter toward that ambiguous edge where recognition gives way to fear.

Horns are one of the most direct archetypal markers of the Namahage mask. From the earliest depictions of oni in Japanese folklore to the devils painted on European church walls, they announce a figure that has crossed out of the human realm. Horns signal that what stands before you is part beast, part spirit, something armed by nature itself. In Japanese tales, oni are almost never without them. The curve of a horn instantly locates the Namahage in that lineage, recognizable to every villager before a word is spoken.

But the power of horns is not only symbolic. In the low interior of an Akita farmhouse, they become physical presences. The body of the Namahage is enlarged by them, the room itself seems smaller, and the family suddenly feels crowded by a shape that should not fit indoors. For children especially, the horns mark the intruder as threatening.

The symbolism carries further still. Horns are dangerous, but they are also defenses. A horned animal cannot easily be hunted or handled; it commands distance and respect. To confront a horned figure at your threshold is to be reminded that what has entered is not tame, not safe, and not easily dismissed. At the same time, horns can suggest guardianship, the same force that terrifies children also promises to keep evil outside the door. That double edge, both threat and shield, is part of their power.

In the Namahage ritual, horns achieve all of these things at once. They declare that the visitor is not human, they enlarge the mask's silhouette until it dominates the space, and they remind the household that they face something armed by nature and by tradition. For a child, to look up and see horns is to feel suddenly small, fragile, and subject to a force that cannot be resisted. The archetype is simple, ancient, and effective: horns mean otherness, danger, and authority.

Equally important is the transformation the mask brings to the wearer. To put on the Namahage mask is not merely to conceal one's face but to adopt an entirely new identity, one that permits actions otherwise impossible. A young man in the village cannot shout at children or scold elders in daily life. Once the mask is tied, he not only can, he must. The role requires him to thunder through houses, demand obedience, and frighten without apology.

This transformation is what gives the ritual its force. Families do not simply hear a neighbor's son yelling; they hear the Namahage. The man inside becomes secondary, almost irrelevant. What matters is that the mask authorizes him, pushing him across the boundary between ordinary villager and ritual figure. In that moment, the mask is not costume but license.

Such transformative power is not unique to Oga. Across the world, masks have served as permission to invert roles and suspend normal rules. Carnival traditions in Europe allowed peasants to mock lords and priests. Spirit dances in Africa gave masked figures the authority of ancestors. In Japan itself, shrine festivals often use masks to shift performers into roles of gods or demons. The Namahage belongs to this pattern. It makes the wearer into an archetype, a figure who temporarily steps outside everyday life in order to enforce, paradoxically, the discipline of everyday life.

The threshold has always been a charged space: the line between inside and outside, between family and stranger, between safety and exposure. In rural Akita, that line is marked by the genkan, the narrow entryway where boots are removed and snow is shaken off. It is here that the Namahage mask makes its most powerful appearance. Its exaggerated features are not meant for open streets or wide spaces but for this moment of compression, when the demon suddenly fills the doorway and the household realizes that what was private is now exposed.

Anthropologists often speak of liminality in ritual, the experience of being between states, no longer what you were but not yet what you will be. The Namahage mask embodies this perfectly. It is a human face that is not human, a villager who is not a villager. The moment it appears at the threshold, the family itself is drawn into liminality. They are no longer simply eating their meal by the fire. They have crossed into another state: participants in a ritual drama of accusation, negotiation, and renewal.

The physical setting matters. The doorway is narrow, the ceiling low, the fire behind the family casting shadows that make the horns and brows loom larger still. The Namahage does not stand politely on the step; it pushes forward, snow on its shoulders, breath steaming in the cold air of the genkan. The threshold becomes a stage, and the mask is the prop that makes the performance real. Without it, the intrusion would be only noise. With it, the intrusion becomes judgment.

The archetypal power of the mask explains why it endures so vividly in memory. Ask an adult in Oga about their childhood, and they may not recall the exact words shouted or the bargains struck at the hearth. What they remember, always, is the face. They remember the eyes fixed in perpetual stare, the horns, the painted surface that seemed alive in firelight.

This is not chance. The mask was designed to leave that mark. Human memory is drawn most strongly to what is seen and what is felt, and the Namahage delivers both at once. A carved face, exaggerated beyond the human, presented at the most vulnerable moment of childhood, fuses terror with clarity.

Even decades later, adults can describe with precision the mask that leaned through the doorway, though the voices and words have blurred away.

The lesson survives because form is stronger than detail. Children may forget the exact threat, but they do not forget the unblinking gaze or the wide, fanged mouth. The image itself becomes the vessel of discipline, carried forward in memory long after the ritual has ended. In this way the Namahage mask works not only in the moment but across a lifetime. It ensures that fear is remembered as vividly as any story, and that the authority of the mask continues long after the horns and straw have been packed away.

Section 5: Conclusion

The Namahage mask is more than carved wood, paint, or straw. It is a vessel of fear, yes, but also of memory, discipline, and continuity. It replaces the person with a role, so the voice that speaks is the mask's authority rather than a neighbor's opinion. Its horns announce danger and strength, enlarging the figure until it is too large for the room it enters. Its sudden intrusion at the threshold transforms an ordinary farmhouse doorway into a stage for judgment. And its endurance in memory proves its deepest power: even when the voices fade and the details blur, the mask itself remains clear, carried across decades in the minds of those who saw it as children.

To carve such a mask is to join an unbroken chain of labor. The artisan does not simply fashion an object for display; he renews a tradition. The horned demon of Oga recalls horned figures in Europe, grotesque gargoyles in cathedrals, and open-mouthed guardian statues at Buddhist temples. Fear carved into wood is a language spoken in many places, yet the cedar cut from local slopes, the chisel passed down in a village workshop, the snow melting from the shoulders of the performer, these make the Namahage unmistakably of Oga. The mask is both universal and particular, at once an archetype recognized across cultures and the face of a community that has lived with harsh winters for centuries.

What sets the Namahage apart is its double existence. By itself, the mask is an artifact: something to admire for its sharp lines and glossy lacquer. But in the hands of a performer, in the doorway of a farmhouse, it is alive. It does not exist to be looked at but to act. A mask is not finished when the carving is done or the paint dries. It is finished only when it is worn, when its eyes stare and its mouth roars and its horns menace. A museum can preserve the object, but only the ritual preserves the force.

That force is communal. Children tremble before it, because they sense a being larger than themselves. Adults bow before it, because they know it carries the weight of shared memory and obligation. Carvers labor over it, because they know their work will outlast them, entering homes long after they are gone. In every case, the mask fuses human craft with something larger, binding the living to each other and to those who came before.

The lesson is reinforced each winter. Costumes wear out, voices change, performers grow old and step aside, but the mask carries forward. It can be lifted from one face and strapped to another, and the transformation is instant. The same demon that terrified a father can terrify his son. This continuity is not decorative; it is survival. In a land where winter once tested every household, the Namahage mask served as a reminder that vigilance, discipline, and obedience were not optional but necessary. Fear was a teacher, and the mask was its face.

To encounter a Namahage mask, then, is to confront layers of meaning at once. It is the face of a demon, fierce and unrelenting. It is the face of a craftsman, his hand visible in every cut of the chisel. It is the face of a community, demanding discipline through ritual. And it is the face of humanity's oldest archetypes, echoing the horned figures and gaping mouths that appear wherever people have sought to give form to fear.

That is why the mask endures. Not because it is beautiful, though many are. Not because it is rare, though each is unique. It endures because it works. It frightens. It disciplines. It transforms. It bridges generations. It ensures that fear, controlled, ritualized, made visible, continues to teach what words alone cannot.

The Namahage mask is therefore not only a face of fear but a face of necessity. When it appears in the doorway, it is not just a demon entering the home but the community itself, reminding its members of what must be remembered. To bow before it is to acknowledge that survival has always required respect for fear. And to carve it, wear it, or face it is to take part in continuity itself, an old lesson carried forward year after year, carved again into cedar, painted again in fire and ice, and remembered long after the snow has melted.

CHAPTER 5: The Ritual Garb: Straw and Embodiment

Section 1: Straw as Material and Symbol

The mask is the most immediately striking element of the Namahage, but without the straw costume the figure would never carry the same presence. It is the straw body that transforms a villager into a hulking, unfamiliar being, one that crackles when it moves and leaves a trail of stalks behind as if the fields themselves have been pulled indoors. To understand the Namahage costume, one has to understand straw in the context of northern Japan: where it comes from, how it has been used, and what it means.

In Akita Prefecture, rice has long been both lifeblood and burden. The climate makes cultivation difficult, the winters long and punishing, the summers humid but brief. Every harvest demanded enormous labor, and every grain carried with it a measure of survival for the village. Straw, the byproduct of this harvest, was never waste. It was twisted into rope, woven into sandals, shaped into baskets and mats, used for thatching and for the cores of tatami. To dress a figure in straw was to clothe it in the residue of the year's labor, the material that lingered after the rice had been threshed and stored.

The straw coats worn by the Namahage are locally called kede, a mino-style rain cape particular to Oga. Across rural Japan, straw rain capes (mino) once kept farmers and fishermen dry, layered over cotton or hemp; in Oga, households wove kede each winter from rice straw and replaced them as they wore out. They were practical, cheap, and renewable, built each season from the most abundant local material, and everyone read them as the residue of fieldwork. By the time the Namahage rite settled into its present form, the kede had come to stand for labor itself, the cycle of planting, harvest, and repair. On a Namahage's body the same garment changes register: no longer workwear but a uniform of inspection, the field come inside to demand an accounting.

The cultural meaning of straw extends beyond practicality. In Shinto tradition, straw has long been associated with purity and with the threshold between human and divine. Sacred ropes, shimenawa, are woven from rice straw and hung at shrines to mark spaces where spirits dwell. They appear above doorways, around sacred trees, even across temporary festival stages. The material carries connotations of protection, warding, and renewal. When villagers wrap their young men in straw coats and send them into homes as Namahage, they are clothing them in something both ordinary and charged with spiritual association.

Straw also embodies impermanence. A straw coat cannot last more than a season. Rain soaks it, snow weighs it down, friction wears it to tatters. To build a Namahage costume is to acknowledge that it will disintegrate almost immediately, leaving trails on floors, breaking down in the cold. That fragility is part of its meaning. The ritual is renewed each year because the materials demand it. The masks may endure for decades, but the straw must be gathered again, cut, bundled, and tied anew. This constant renewal links the Namahage directly to the cycles of agriculture. As rice returns, as snow melts, as fields are planted and harvested, so too is the costume remade.

The symbolism deepens when one considers the season of the ritual. The Namahage appear at New Year's, a moment when the community seeks purification and renewal. The straw they wear is residue of the old year, taken from harvest and labor past. To bring that material into the house is to bring the year's labor to the threshold one final time, but in transformed form. The straw body is no longer a farmer bent over a field but a demon demanding promises. It is both reminder and warning: you have worked hard, but idleness can undo you, and the land does not forgive laziness.

Descriptions of the costume emphasize its bulk and its awkwardness. Layers of straw are tied around the torso and limbs until the human form underneath is obscured. The result is a shape that rustles when it moves, that spills fragments of itself as it turns, that makes the air seem filled with husks and fibers. The material has its own smell, a mixture of field dust and dry stalk, that contrasts with the interior of the home. For children, this is part of the shock. The familiar room suddenly smells like the outside. The ordinary air becomes charged with the scent of the harvest transformed into a monster's skin.

Straw also adds sound to the ritual. As the Namahage shift their weight, straw rubs against straw with a dry rasp. When they pass through a doorway, the bundles catch on wood and shed fragments with a pattering noise. Each step on tatami presses the stalks into the weave with a texture different from cloth. Parents who recount their memories of childhood visits often recall the sound of straw brushing their shoulders, a sound both harmless and terrifying because it carried with it the full presence of the demon.

The choice of straw can be seen as inevitable in a place like Oga. It was the most available material, renewable each year, already tied to both labor and ritual. But inevitability should not obscure meaning. The Namahage costume works because straw does more than cover a body. It connects the figure to the land, to the harvest, and to the fragile line between plenty and famine. The children who trembled before the straw demons understood, even if only in their bones, that those stalks came from the same fields their parents bent over in summer. The demons were clothed in the proof of survival, and to be judged by them was to be judged by the year itself.

Ethnographers who have studied the Namahage often note how inseparable the costume is from the performance. A mask alone does not terrify in the same way. A mask can be handled, turned over, recognized as wood. A straw body fills a room. It changes the air, it leaves traces, it rustles in a way that feels alive. In some villages, elders described the Namahage less as demons and more as the embodiment of the field itself coming to check on the household. This interpretation may not be universal, but it captures an important truth: the costume does not disguise a man, it animates the land.

In modern times, when synthetic costumes and simplified versions sometimes appear at tourist demonstrations, villagers are quick to insist that straw is not optional. To lose the straw is to lose the essence of the ritual. Cloth costumes may be easier to manage, less messy, more durable, but they cannot carry the same weight. The ritual depends on the mess, the fragments, the way straw sticks to hair and clothes, the way the floor must be swept after the visit. These traces remind the family that the visit truly occurred, that something larger than themselves entered and left behind evidence.

The symbolism of straw in Namahage performance can also be read in light of broader Japanese aesthetics. In art and poetry, straw often represents transience, the seasonality of life, the fleetingness of human effort against nature. Haiku poets wrote of straw huts buried in snow, of straw sandals wearing thin on long journeys, of straw effigies burned in rituals to carry away misfortune. The Namahage costume gathers all of these associations and binds them into a single terrifying presence. It is both protection and threat, both ordinary byproduct and extraordinary embodiment.

The most striking feature of the straw costume may be the way it erases individuality. A man in ordinary clothing remains himself, recognizable to neighbors even under a mask. A man wrapped in layers of straw becomes a figure without clear outline, a bulk that no longer moves like a farmer or fisherman. The straw redefines posture, exaggerates gestures, muffles or amplifies sound. In this way, the costume finishes what the mask begins: it strips away the personal and replaces it with archetype. The Namahage is not a villager pretending to be a demon. It is a demon wearing the village's harvest, moving with the authority of centuries.

To see the Namahage in straw is to see the harvest returned in another form. The rice that sustained the village has given not only food but also the material for terror and discipline. The stalks that bent under autumn sun now loom over children in the glow of winter lamps. The same material that once lay in the fields as passive crop now enters homes as active presence. This transformation is the heart of the costume's meaning.

The straw body of the Namahage is at once practical, symbolic, and aesthetic. It is practical because it uses the most abundant local material. It is symbolic because it ties the ritual to labor, purity, and renewal. It is aesthetic because it creates a figure that is both overwhelming and unforgettable. To reduce it to any one of these would be to miss the complexity of the costume. The Namahage are terrifying not only because of their masks, but because of the way straw itself has been transformed into skin, voice, and authority.

Section 2: Sound, Bulk, and Silhouette

When the Namahage enters a home, the first thing the eye seizes is the mask. The face shocks, but the impression of terror would fade quickly if it were not carried by a body that feels larger than any ordinary man. The costume of straw provides this amplification. It gives scale, sound, and outline, making the Namahage appear not as a neighbor in disguise but as a force pressing into the family's space. The costume is less about hiding the man than about transforming him into something that could not exist outside ritual.

The bulk of the costume is the most immediate effect. Ordinary coats or robes follow the lines of the body, revealing shoulders, elbows, knees. Straw does not. Bundled and tied, the stalks radiate outward, rounding edges, thickening limbs, and blurring joints. A slim youth disappears into the costume, his build erased beneath layers that make his arms into beams and his legs into stanchions. The torso becomes a block, square and uneven, its proportions exaggerated beyond recognition. Inside the low rooms of traditional Oga farmhouses, where ceiling beams often hung only a head's height above the floor, this bulk was overwhelming. When a Namahage straightened to full height, his shoulders seemed to strain against the architecture itself, as though the building could barely contain him.

The weight of the costume adds to the impression. Straw is light when dry, but once bound in dense layers and dampened by snow, it hangs heavy. To move in it requires force, and that force translates into a style of movement that is abrupt and emphatic. Steps are not delicate. They are broad, stamping, shaking free snow from sleeves and sending fragments of straw raining onto the tatami. The costume demands that its wearer become imposing, because only an imposing gait can manage its resistance. What the children saw, then, was not just a bulked figure but a bulk that moved as though it meant to crush the space it entered.

Sound completes the impression. Straw is never silent. Each shift of weight sends stalks brushing and rasping against one another, a dry whisper that builds into a steady crackle as the figure paces the room. The motion of the arms, with their long straw sleeves, produces a swish that is distinct from cloth or fur. When the Namahage brushes against the doorframe, the stalks catch and snap, releasing small fragments that patter onto the floor. Oral recollections often emphasize this sound. Adults remembering their childhood visits describe not only the roar of voices but the constant background of rustle and crack, as if the figure carried the fields inside and spread their noise across the house. The auditory presence of the Namahage is inseparable from its costume.

For children, the sound was sometimes worse than the sight. A mask can be avoided by looking away. Eyes can be shut against painted horns and teeth. But ears cannot be closed. Even when hiding behind a parent's sleeve, the child still heard the hiss of straw over wood, the scrape of stalks along the tatami, the sudden burst when a sleeve dragged a spray of straw loose. The sound pursued them in the dark corners of the room, making it impossible to escape the sense of proximity.

Silhouette carries another dimension of fear. In firelight or lamplight, a straw-clad figure casts shadows that no longer resemble a man. The uneven outline, with fringes and tufts, produces shapes that crawl across the walls like multiple bodies. Horns lengthen or distort depending on angle, and the long sleeves trail into the dark like limbs too long to be human. Against the white of a snowy doorway, the figure appears shaggy, undefined, like a beast that has shaken itself free of the mountain and stumbled down into the village. The vagueness is itself a form of terror. Children could not map the shape onto the familiar. A neighbor in ordinary clothes remains a man, but a neighbor in straw becomes an ungraspable outline, unmoored from known categories.

The costume also creates touch, whether deliberate or accidental. When a straw sleeve brushes a child's arm, the sensation is prickly, dry, and unfamiliar indoors. One woman interviewed in later life remembered the scrape of straw across her cheek more vividly than any shouted question. She recalled that the mask's face could be avoided by looking away, but the straw found her no matter how she turned. This contact was harmless but unforgettable, the body's memory of the field suddenly intruding on the skin. For many, it was this mingling of fear and touch that marked the ritual most deeply.

All of these effects, the bulk that fills a room, the rustle that never ceases, the silhouette that distorts, combine into an atmosphere of assault on the senses. The mask provides the initial shock, but the straw ensures that the experience cannot be contained to the eyes alone. The ritual works precisely because the costume surrounds the family with texture, sound, and motion. To be visited by the Namahage is to have one's entire perceptual field disrupted. The ordinary home is overwhelmed by bulk that presses against beams, sound that fills the corners, straw that litters the floor.

What makes the effect so striking is the paradox at its heart. Straw is fragile. It crumbles, sheds, and burns easily. A child could pull a stalk free with no effort. Yet bound together and animated in ritual, the same material becomes terrifying. This inversion reinforces the lesson of the Namahage. Idleness and fragility can turn deadly when ignored. The flimsy becomes overwhelming when multiplied, just as small acts of laziness can build into ruin. The straw body is not only a disguise but also a metaphor, a visible reminder of how the weakest material, properly arranged, can dominate a space.

The community understood this transformation intuitively. Parents who swept up straw fragments after the visit often described the floor as looking as if the field had scattered itself indoors. The mess was evidence of the ritual's reality, a trace left behind to remind the family of what had occurred. Children who found straw in their hair or clothes the next day carried with them a physical reminder of their encounter. The costume's bulk and sound thus extended beyond the moment, persisting in fragments that outlasted the roar of the masks.

By focusing on bulk, rustle, and silhouette, one can see how the Namahage costume shifts the ritual from performance to environment. It is not only a man in straw entering a house. It is the house itself being altered, filled with new sounds, new shapes, new sensations. The straw does not decorate the figure. It transforms the entire space. Fear is not limited to the mask's face; it is woven into every movement, every rasp, every shadow. That is why the costume cannot be replaced by cloth or synthetic imitation without loss. The straw is not just material. It is the medium of the ritual's power.

Section 3: Transformation of the Wearer

The Namahage is feared for what it represents, but the ritual only works because the men behind the masks allow themselves to be transformed. To wear the costume is not simply to put on a disguise. It is to step out of ordinary time, to abandon one's given name, one's place in the family, one's role in the village, and to speak as something beyond the human. The straw and mask are instruments, but their power is completed in the body and mind of the wearer.

Accounts from men who have taken the role often begin with the preparation. The costume is heavy, awkward, and prickly. The straw sleeves scratch the arms, the weight on the shoulders presses down, and the mask is hot and hard to see through. Breathing grows difficult as condensation gathers behind the wood, and speech is muffled into a distorted roar. These discomforts matter less than the effect: the more encumbered the man feels, the less like himself he becomes. His reflection disappears; his voice emerges altered. What he sees of the room through narrow slits is already framed as otherworldly. The physical reality initiates the mental shift.

Anonymity is crucial. In a small village, every face is known. Children recognize cousins, neighbors, apprentices by their gestures and speech. The mask interrupts this recognition. A boy who would never dare raise his voice to an elder suddenly finds himself roaring at an entire household, his words carrying authority. The anonymity releases him from the rules of hierarchy. Within the costume, he is not himself; he is Namahage. The license to transgress is part of the exhilaration. For a brief night, the social order is inverted, and the young, normally the least powerful, become vessels of command.

This transformation does not only elevate the wearer's status but changes his manner. A young man unused to speaking publicly finds his voice amplified, his movements larger, his body restless with energy. Oral histories describe how men rehearsed their lines in low voices beforehand but found that once the mask was on, the words came out as shouts, louder than they thought possible. The costume encouraged exaggeration, demanded force. Movements that might have been self-conscious became expansive. Fearlessness took hold, not because the man had lost his doubts, but because those doubts were hidden under layers of straw.

The transformation also carried responsibility. To be Namahage was not playacting. The wearer knew that children's memories of the night would last for decades. He had to balance terror with ritual, improvisation with tradition. Too little energy would weaken the effect; too much cruelty would leave scars. The young men learned from older peers, from whispered advice and observation, how to strike the right balance. Many remembered their first time as a mixture of thrill and weight: the thrill of power, the weight of carrying the community's ritual on their shoulders. In some villages, elders watched closely, correcting or restraining a novice if his performance wandered too far into farce or menace.

The costume amplified not only the body but the inner life. To feel one's breath roaring unnaturally through the mask was to feel taken over by something outside oneself. Men spoke of forgetting their own names, of becoming absorbed into the role. The ritual's continuity reinforced this. Each year, the Namahage returned, not as individuals, but as the same figures, unchanged. A boy who saw them at seven would see them again at eight, at nine, always as the same horned strangers. When he grew old enough to wear the costume himself, he did not replace someone. He became what had always been. The transformation was not substitution but incarnation.

For some, the experience lingered long after the straw was shed. Former participants described the exhilaration of being free from self-consciousness, of speaking with a voice that carried weight, of embodying fear and respect. Others recalled the exhaustion, the scratches, the aching shoulders, the relief of taking off the mask. Both memories underscored the distance between self and role. To wear the costume was to enter a state impossible to maintain in daily life, but unforgettable once lived.

This transformation also illuminated the ritual's purpose. If the Namahage had been played by outsiders, actors, performers, the effect would have faltered. Its strength came from the paradox: the men behind the masks were neighbors, yet on this night they were not. The costume allowed them to dissolve into archetypes, to carry the voice of the ancestors, the mountains, the sea. The children believed because the wearers believed, at least for the space of the night. Fear depended on conviction. Without transformation, there would be no ritual, only theater.

From the perspective of the community, the transformation was a rite of passage. Young men proved themselves not only by frightening children but by accepting the burden of embodying tradition. They learned endurance under discomfort, self-control under anonymity, and the power of voice when channeled through ritual. Participation prepared them for adulthood, where authority would return to them in more ordinary ways. The mask was a rehearsal for responsibility.

Psychologically, the act blurred the line between human and spirit. In anthropological terms, the costume induced a liminal state. The wearer left behind ordinary identity, entered a transitional role as Namahage, and returned the next day to normal life. This liminality was essential to the ritual's power. It reassured the community that boundaries could be crossed and reestablished, that order could be disrupted and then restored. The transformation of the wearer was the mechanism by which the transformation of the household was achieved.

The final act of removing the costume was not trivial. After the visits, men returned to a gathering place, stripped off straw, set masks aside, and reemerged as themselves. The relief was mixed with quiet pride. They had carried the role, embodied the figure, preserved the ritual. For a few hours, they had been more than individuals. They had been the Namahage, the visitors at the door, the voice of fear and discipline. In those hours, they had ceased to be themselves, and in doing so, reminded the village of what survival required.

The costume, then, is not only a shell of straw and wood. It is a threshold for the wearer, a device that takes a young man across the boundary of self into a communal role larger than any individual. Without that transformation, the ritual would falter. With it, the Namahage live, not as men in disguise, but as presences that shake the walls, unsettle the heart, and leave behind a memory that no child or parent can ignore.

Section 4: Parallels with European Ritual Dress

The Namahage is deeply rooted in the Oga Peninsula, but when placed beside the rituals of other agrarian cultures, its form looks less isolated. Across Europe, in regions equally shaped by harsh winters and subsistence farming, villagers have long sent masked figures into their homes and streets at the turning of the year. These figures, like the Namahage, are shaggy, loud, overwhelming, and designed to turn neighbors temporarily into something more than human. The comparison does not diminish the uniqueness of the Japanese tradition. Instead, it situates Namahage within a larger human pattern: the use of costume to embody fear and renewal.

The most obvious parallel is the Krampus of the Alpine regions, especially Austria and southern Germany. Krampus appears during December, shadowing the more benevolent St. Nicholas. While Nicholas rewards good behavior with gifts, Krampus embodies the opposite. His costume is made of heavy furs, thick and coarse, that expand the wearer's size. A wooden mask, usually painted black or red, bears horns, fangs, and a grotesque expression. Chains are wrapped around the body, and bells hang from belts, clanging with each movement. The performance involves chasing children, brandishing switches, and filling the streets with sound. The similarity to Namahage lies not only in the mask but in the way costume and noise combine to overwhelm. Both figures rely on bulk and constant sound to make them inescapable. Krampus rattles chains; Namahage sheds straw and stamps on wood. In both cases, the visitor's presence is impossible to ignore because it saturates sight, sound, and touch.

In Bulgaria, the Kukeri fulfill a related function. These masked men appear in late winter, wearing costumes made from shaggy animal skins, sometimes layered until the figure looks more beast than human. Their faces are covered with elaborately carved masks, painted in bright colors, often crowned with horns or feathers. Around their waists hang enormous cowbells, each weighing several kilograms. As they dance through villages, the bells create a constant thunder, a wall of sound meant to frighten away evil spirits and ensure fertility for the coming year. The Kukeri are not directed at children in the same way as Namahage, yet the mechanics are similar. They take the materials of ordinary life, skins from livestock, bells from herds, and repurpose them into instruments of awe and dread. Like the Namahage, their performance is communal, seasonal, and understood not as entertainment but as necessity. Winter must be confronted, and noise, bulk, and masks are the chosen weapons.

On the Italian island of Sardinia, the Mamuthones of Mamoiada form another striking echo. Their costumes consist of heavy black wooden masks, dark woolen garments, and sheepskins. Most distinctive are the bells strapped to their backs, dozens of them arranged in layers that can weigh more than thirty kilograms. As the Mamuthones march in processions, they move in synchronized steps, making the bells sound together with a deep, metallic rhythm. The effort required is immense; participants stagger under the load. Yet the very burden is part of the transformation. The men cease to be individuals and become a collective mass of sound and weight, trudging figures whose identity is erased by costume. Here again, the parallels to

Namahage are clear. Straw may not weigh as much as bells, but when soaked with snow and layered thick, it creates the same sense of encumbrance, demanding a change in posture and movement. In both cases, the costume enforces transformation, making the wearer into something other than himself.

What links these traditions is the way ordinary rural materials become the substance of fear. Straw, fur, skins, bells, these are not exotic imports but the byproducts of subsistence economies. The villagers used what was at hand, yet by layering and exaggerating these materials, they created figures that seemed to emerge from beyond the human world. There is a practical genius in this. The same stalks that covered roofs and fed livestock became the body of demons. The same bells that marked herds became instruments of dread. Ritual did not depend on wealth or distant trade; it grew directly from the landscape and its labors.

The psychological effect is also consistent across cultures. Children everywhere know the difference between stories and realities. A tale can be ignored, but a figure that enters the home, larger than life, shedding fragments onto the floor, cannot be dismissed. When the Krampus lashes chains against the ground or the Mamuthones thunder in unison, the sound reverberates in the chest. When the Namahage fills the room with straw rustling and shadows, the fear is equally physical. It bypasses reason and impresses itself directly onto the body. This is what makes the memory last. No amount of parental scolding carries the same weight as an encounter with a figure that seems to emerge from beyond the ordinary world.

Despite their differences, these rituals share a common logic. They take place in winter or at the year's turn, when communities are most vulnerable to scarcity and uncertainty. They use fear not to paralyze but to discipline, to remind, to renew. They mark the boundary between one year and the next, between survival and failure, between order and disorder. The figures are frightening, but they are also protective, ensuring that children remember their duties and that adults recall their responsibilities. They are, in this sense, guardians as much as monsters.

The parallels suggest that humanity, when faced with harsh climates and fragile economies, independently discovered the same solution: create a figure that embodies fear, dress it in the materials of everyday survival, and send it into the community to shock people back into vigilance. Namahage is one such figure, but not the only one. To recognize this is not to flatten its uniqueness but to understand its deeper significance. It is a local expression of a universal human strategy: to ritualize fear so that it becomes a tool rather than a threat.

For the people of Oga, the Namahage did not belong to Europe. They were born of Japanese soil, Japanese winters, Japanese deities and demons. Yet when one listens to the rustle of straw in a farmhouse and compares it to the clanging bells of Sardinia or the chains of Austria, the kinship is unmistakable. The world has many ways of summoning demons, but the reasons are the same. Fear, when channeled through ritual, keeps communities awake to their duties and aware of their fragility. It is a language older than writing, spoken in costumes, in sound, and in shadows that outgrow the human form.

Section 5: Reflection and Closing

The Namahage mask draws the first attention, but the costume is what makes the figure fully present. A mask alone could be hung on a wall or set on a shelf. It could be studied as an artifact, admired as carving, feared in its frozen stare. But when it is tied to a body wrapped in straw, widened with bulk, set rustling and dripping snow in the dark of a farmhouse, it becomes something more than object. The costume makes the demon walk. It makes the visit possible. It fills the room not just with sight but with sound, smell, weight, and heat. Without it, the Namahage would be a face. With it, the Namahage is a body that no one can ignore.

This body is not fixed. It is rebuilt each year from the fields. Straw is gathered after harvest, dried, bundled, and then fashioned into coats, skirts, sleeves, hoods. Each strand was once stalk, bending in the summer wind, then cut and threshed for grain. What remains after food is taken becomes costume. In this sense the Namahage enters the house clothed not in something foreign, but in the village itself. He wears the residue of labor, the material that holds the memory of planting and harvest. When he rustles across the floor, it is as if the fields themselves have entered, demanding acknowledgment. Fear is woven from the same substance as survival.

For the wearer, the costume blurs identity. It thickens the outline, muffles the voice, conceals the familiar body. The villager becomes a figure that cannot be mistaken for any one person. Anonymity allows transformation. But the straw is more than disguise. Its weight and scratch reshape posture, its sound accompanies each gesture, its smell declares its presence. To wear straw is to move differently, to feel oneself no longer as an individual but as something rougher, heavier, closer to the earth. This change is what lets a young man shout at children, command parents, and speak as if his words carried ancestral authority. The costume permits him to stop being himself for a night and take up the role of something greater.

For the children, the costume is unforgettable. What remains in memory is not only the painted face but the sensation of straw brushing their skin, the rasp in the dark when the demon leaned close, the pieces left behind on tatami like evidence of intrusion. Straw on the floor was proof that the visitor was real, that the fear was not a dream. Even decades later, adults recalling their childhood speak of the sound first: the rustle, the scratch, the sudden closeness of a texture usually confined to barns and fields. That sensory memory becomes the lasting proof that they once faced the Namahage directly.

The costume's impermanence is part of its meaning. Masks are carved to endure; some have lasted generations. Straw, by contrast, is perishable. It frays, grows brittle, falls away in use. After the night's visits, the fragments are swept up and burned, or tossed aside, or fed to the fire. The next year new straw is cut and tied, and the body of the Namahage is rebuilt. This cycle of decay and renewal mirrors the ritual itself. Each year laziness returns, disobedience returns, fear must be rekindled, promises must be made again. Just as there is no permanent costume, there is no permanent discipline. Both must be renewed with the turn of the year. The fragility of straw underscores the fragility of human resolve.

In this way the costume also carries a philosophy. It reminds the village that nothing is finished. Grain harvested one year must be planted the next. Promises made in December must be kept through winter and spring, then remade when weakness returns. Fear must be confronted again and again. The costume embodies this lesson: it is woven for a moment, powerful in that moment, then undone, only to be woven again. Continuity comes not from permanence but from repetition.

There is also a generational rhythm in the costume. The children who once hid from the rustling figure grow into young men who wear the same straw. The memory of fear becomes the responsibility of causing fear. In this sense, the costume is not just clothing but inheritance. To tie it on is to accept a role passed down from elders, a role that will in turn be handed to those younger still. The rustle heard in childhood becomes the rustle one makes in adulthood. The transformation is complete when the memory of hiding behind a parent shifts into the experience of looming above a child. The costume is the bridge across which each generation walks from one side of the ritual to the other.

Symbolically, the straw coat makes visible the connection between labor and discipline. Straw is the byproduct of toil in the fields. It is what remains after sustenance has been taken. To wear it as a demon is to carry the field into the home, to remind everyone that survival is tied to effort. Laziness is not simply a moral failing; it is a threat to the household's ability to endure winter. The rustle of straw in the room is a reminder that life comes from labor, that neglect endangers all. The costume makes this truth unavoidable. It surrounds the child with the very material that testifies to the work of the year. The demon's body is built of what laziness would waste.

The closing image of the costume is always absence. After the night, the straw is gone, the masks stored, the house swept. What remains is memory: the sound of rustling sleeves, the silhouette filling the doorway, the sensation of being pressed upon by something larger than oneself. The costume does not endure as object; it endures as impression. It does not belong in a museum case or a collector's shelf. It belongs in the mind, in the body, in the small shiver that comes with recollection. That is its true strength. It is not meant to last as material. It is meant to last as memory.

When the Namahage leaves, the household returns to itself. Children are comforted, parents settle again into ordinary roles. But the straw has already done its work. It has embodied discipline, carried the fields inside, transformed men into figures of fear, and reminded the community that survival depends on vigilance. The costume is gone, but what it created remains. It is in the straighter posture of a child the next morning, in the more attentive hands of a parent, in the village that feels once more bound together by shared encounter. The straw coat is fragile, but its meaning is not. Each year it reappears, each year it vanishes, and each year it leaves behind the same lesson: that fear, when ritualized, is not an enemy but a teacher, woven from the fields, carried on the shoulders, and shed onto the floor to remind the living of their duties.

CHAPTER 6: Implements of Authority

Section 1: Introduction

The Namahage does not arrive empty-handed. Mask and straw define its appearance, but implements give it force. Without them the figure could still be frightening, but it would lack weight, the sense that something more than shouting and posturing has entered the room. Implements extend the demon's presence beyond his body, adding reach, sound, and the possibility of consequence. A mask may terrify, but a mask coupled with a knife, a bucket, or a book creates the impression of judgment carried out.

These tools are not exotic inventions. They are drawn from the ordinary stores of a fishing and farming community: kitchen knives, wooden pails, ledgers, purification wands. Their very familiarity makes them powerful. A child who sees a straw-coated figure clutching a massive wooden knife cannot dismiss it as a prop; the child knows knives are kept in the kitchen, sharp enough to gut fish or slice daikon. To see such an object in the grip of a demon figure magnifies its menace. What is normally used for survival is suddenly reimagined as an instrument of punishment.

Each household knows the implements by sight. Each implement carries layers of meaning shaped by daily life. The oke pail is for water or rice, but in the hands of a Namahage it threatens to carry off a child. The ledger, harmless in an elder's keeping, becomes terrifying when brandished as evidence of misbehavior. The implements do not need to draw blood or perform purification; they only need to be held in demon hands for the imagination to do the rest. Implements turn ritual into theater, and theater into memory.

The most iconic of these objects, and the one most consistently associated with the Namahage, is the wooden knife.

Section 2: The Wooden Knife (Deba-bōchō or Namahage-bōchō)

The knife is typically oversized. In Oga it is called the deba-bōchō, after the thick-bladed kitchen knives used to prepare fish, but the Namahage version is exaggerated in both length and width. Some are carved as long as a child's arm, their edges dulled, their weight enough to make them unwieldy in actual use. They are often painted black or left as raw wood, handles wrapped roughly in cloth or cord. There is no mistaking their shape. Even dulled and oversized, they read immediately as knives.

The visual power of the blade lies in its scale. A kitchen knife is an ordinary sight on a cutting board, but when multiplied to twice or three times its size, it becomes something symbolic, even mythic. In the tight space of a farmhouse entryway, such a knife seems to swallow the room, filling the air between demon and child with the possibility of being cut down. The blade glints in firelight, the shadow of its edge stretching along the tatami. Children stare at it before they dare to meet the mask's eyes.

Historically, the knife connects to labor. Oga was a fishing region as much as a farming one, and knives were indispensable. Every household relied on them to gut cod, slice squid, and carve vegetables in the long winter months when stews and pickles sustained life. To exaggerate the knife in the hand of a Namahage was to take the most essential tool of survival and transform it into a weapon of discipline. What fed the family by day could terrify them by night.

The psychological effect is profound. Parents describe how children freeze when the Namahage raises the knife and shouts accusations. The threat is not of actual harm, the community would not tolerate genuine danger, but of symbolic violence. The knife is the instrument with which laziness will be cut away, lies stripped, disobedience excised. In this way, the knife is both physical prop and moral metaphor.

Some scholars see echoes here of ancient purification rituals, where objects symbolized the cutting away of corruption or disease. The Namahage knife may have inherited some of this meaning. But in its lived form, the knife is less about ritual precision than about theatrical intimidation. Children do not analyze its symbolism; they see a blade. That immediacy is the point. The intellect can reflect later, but in the moment, fear must be visceral.

Oral testimonies collected in the twentieth century often emphasize the knife as the most vivid element of the Namahage visit. Again and again, villagers recalled that even after the shouting, pounding, and scattered straw had faded, the sight of the blade endured. People remembered the way it caught the firelight as it lifted, or how its edge seemed to hover unnervingly close to them in the narrow space of the farmhouse. For many, the memory of the knife eclipsed the mask itself: the painted face could be explained away as wood, but the blade, even if wooden, carried the unmistakable form of a weapon. Children clutched their parents, convinced it could slice through floorboards or tatami; adults remembered how the room seemed to contract when the knife was raised, as though the whole household held its breath. Such accounts suggest that the Namahage's most ordinary prop was also its most effective. The knife made the threat tangible, concentrating all of the ritual's accusations into a single, sharp point that the mind could not forget.

The knife also serves the performers. For the young men who take on the role of Namahage, holding a knife alters posture and presence. To grip a long blade requires the whole arm, the shoulders, even the stance. It makes their movements sharper, more deliberate. The knife gives them a prop through which to channel the authority of their role. Without it, they might feel like villagers in costume; with it, they feel like figures to be feared. Implements not only frighten the audience, they strengthen the performer's conviction.

There is an element of play in the knife's use. Some Namahage exaggerate their gestures, brandishing the blade dramatically, thumping it against the floor, pointing it toward the altar or the children. Others use it sparingly, holding it at rest as a silent reminder. This flexibility shows that the knife is not a rigid symbol but part of the living theater, adaptable to personality and circumstance. A quieter demon might let the mask and voice carry the moment; a more aggressive one might make the knife central to the performance.

Importantly, the knife never truly threatens violence. Parents and children both understand that no harm will come, but the possibility is left unspoken, hanging in the air. That possibility is enough. Fear does not require actual danger; it requires only the believable image of danger. The wooden knife, oversized and blunt, fulfills this role perfectly.

In the wider context of Japanese folklore, knives and blades frequently appear as tools of purification and protection. Swords in Shinto shrines symbolize divine authority, while kitchen knives in ritual contexts can cut away impurity. The Namahage knife, though made of wood, participates in this lineage. It is a domestic object elevated to symbolic weapon, connecting the household to broader traditions of purification through cutting.

Children who grow up in Oga know the truth eventually. They see the knife stored in the community center, painted wood dulled by years of handling, edges smoothed by time. But even then, the memory of how it looked in the hand of a demon does not fade. What was once terrifying becomes laughable only in adulthood. In childhood, it was utterly convincing.

When the visit ends, the knife is put away with the masks and straw. It becomes once again just a prop, an object of wood. But the memory of its raised edge remains sharper than its dulled blade. Implements may be ephemeral, but their psychological cut is lasting. The Namahage knife demonstrates this most clearly: a harmless object transformed into an unforgettable symbol of fear and discipline, powerful not for what it could do, but for what it made people imagine.

Section 3: The Bucket (Oke / Pail)

If the wooden knife is the sharp edge of the Namahage, the bucket is its hollow. Knife and bucket often appear together, one to cut, one to contain, but the pairing isn't obligatory. In older explanations the oke's role is to receive what the knife "scrapes off": namomi, the blister of idleness from lingering by the hearth. Whether children imagined laziness itself being taken, or themselves being hauled off, the bucket's emptiness made removal feel real.

The oke itself was an everyday tool of rural households. Made from cedar or cypress staves bound by bamboo hoops, it carried water, rice, or miso, was dipped into baths, and was set beside wells. Its smell of resin and damp wood was as familiar as smoke from the stove. That familiarity gave the bucket its power in the ritual. It was not exotic. It was ordinary, transformed by context. A vessel that usually held the necessities of life now threatened to hold something undesirable, blisters, bad habits, laziness itself.

Folklorists often point out this inversion: the Namahage do not brandish foreign objects, but the very implements of the household, charged with new meaning. In this sense, the bucket operates as a ritual container for removal and purification. Just as water in Shinto rites carries away impurity, so the Namahage's bucket could be imagined to carry away the household's faults. Whether villagers interpreted it literally or symbolically, the effect was the same: fear and correction made tangible in the hollow of wood.

Stories occasionally circulate of children fearing that they themselves might be taken away in the bucket. Elderly villagers, recalling their youth, describe staring at the oke and imagining it as a trap. Parents, too, sometimes leaned into this impression, pleading with the Namahage not to carry the children off. Yet in the older accounts the bucket's explicit function was not abduction, but collection. What it held was the scraped-off blister, or more broadly, the laziness it represented. In that sense the bucket was not a cradle of kidnapping but a portable refuse bin for bad habits. Still, the fact that children conflated those ideas shows how effective the prop was. The hollow space suggested removal, and that suggestion was enough.

The bucket also mattered for what it did, not just what it signified. Young men carrying it often turned it into an instrument. Striking the rim with the wooden knife made a booming, hollow note that reverberated through the farmhouse. Dropping it to the floor let the boards amplify its crash. Rolling it across tatami or planks created a racket of slats and hoops that startled children into shrieks. In a ritual where volume is essential, the oke became a kind of percussion. Its emptiness was its strength: a vessel of resonance, a drum hidden in plain sight.

There was also a practical layer. In some villages, the bucket served to collect small offerings of sake or rice from households. What it threatened to carry out, bad behavior, it might also carry home in the form of gifts. This dual role bound menace and reciprocity together. The oke reminded families of what might be taken, but also gave them a chance to give. When filled with rice wine, it became a vessel of restored goodwill, proof that the ritual was not only about terror but also about reaffirming ties between visitor and household.

Across Japanese tradition, vessels like buckets, tubs, and bowls appear as symbols of containment. In Shinto purification, water in a bucket is used to rinse away impurity. In Buddhist imagery, containers often represent the collection of merit or offerings. The Namahage's bucket participates in this symbolic system, but with an inverted edge: instead of blessings, it threatens to hold faults; instead of gifts for the gods, it seems poised to take away human weakness. This inversion heightened its power. By using a sacred image of containment in a demonic register, the Namahage turned the everyday oke into a ritualized threat.

The symbolism makes fullest sense when knife and bucket are read together. The knife cuts away what is bad; the bucket ensures it does not remain. One threatens the body, the other threatens containment. Together they form a framework of fear: incision and removal, action and consequence. In ritual logic, they mirror a cycle of cleansing, first the scraping away of corruption, then its collection and disposal.

Today, not all Namahage carry buckets, especially in staged performances. The mask and the straw coat are sufficient for spectacle. But in private homes on New Year's Eve, the oke still appears under an arm or swung at the end of a rope. Its presence ties the ritual back to the household, because it was and remains a household tool. That continuity matters. The same kind of vessel that once held well water now holds memory of discipline. To the children who see it, the bucket is not an ordinary pail. It is the hollow of fear itself, waiting, echoing, reminding.

Section 4: The Book (Register of Names)

If the knife embodies force and the bucket removal, then the book embodies knowledge. Few props in the Namahage ritual unsettle children more than the sight of a ledger or scroll tucked under the demon's arm. It suggests that nothing is secret, that every misdeed has already been recorded. Where the knife threatens the body and the bucket threatens capture, the book threatens exposure.

The book is not a universal implement, but where it appears it has strong effect. Sometimes it's an old household ledger, sometimes a handmade booklet with blank pages, sometimes a bound notebook dressed up as an ancient register. It doesn't matter what's inside. What matters is the illusion that there is writing, and that the writing concerns the child standing before the mask.

Japan has long associated writing with authority. Records determine taxes, land boundaries, even obligations to temples and shrines. In a society where oral promise once held sway, the written word came to dominate, carrying weight far beyond speech. For a child in a rural village, seeing the Namahage consult a ledger was akin to seeing the judgment of the entire community in ink. Even if the pages were blank, the authority of the object was undeniable.

Oral testimonies confirm this effect. Adults remembering their childhood visits often speak of the book in hushed tones. One man recalled the way a Namahage flipped its pages slowly before shouting his name, as if the evidence of his laziness were there in black and white. Another remembered the sting of hearing his own name called out, not by a neighbor or parent, but by a horned figure pretending to read it off a page. It was not simply accusation; it was accusation supported by "proof."

The book creates a layered fear: not only that the demons know, but that they have known all along. It denies the child the defense of secrecy. Every chore neglected, every lie told at school might already be inscribed. This transforms the Namahage from a loud intruder into a kind of cosmic accountant, tallying human failings with perfect memory.

For the young men performing, the book provides another dimension of role-play. To flip pages deliberately, to point to a line and shout, to lean close as if confirming a name, these actions dramatize the demon's authority without requiring actual force. The book allows the Namahage to command silence, to slow the pace of the ritual, to build tension before the next roar. In a ritual otherwise filled with noise and motion, the stillness of reading is powerful.

The symbolism runs deeper still. To record something is to make it endure. Memory can fade, but writing fixes blame. In this sense, the Namahage book reflects the community's concern with continuity, the transmission of discipline across generations.

Even if the names are not truly written, the act of pretending enacts the idea that behavior matters enough to be kept in a record. This echoes wider cultural practices in Japan, where families kept household registers, shrines recorded offerings, and officials maintained meticulous documents. The Namahage book is a rural cousin of these practices, a theatrical echo of real authority.

In some villages, the ledger was explicitly tied to threats of reporting. Parents told children that the Namahage would write their names and pass them along to higher authorities, sometimes even the gods. This blurred the line between ritual theater and religious accountability. It made the stakes larger than the household: a misdeed could leave the walls of the home, carried on paper into realms where excuses no longer worked.

Even when children later discovered the truth, that the ledger was blank, or that the names were scrawled at random, the fear endured. The impression of having been "known" lingers longer than the knowledge of trickery. Adults may laugh about how easily they were fooled, but their stories prove the lasting psychological power of the book.

The book also represents one of the subtler dynamics of shame culture. In a society where appearance and reputation matter as much as private morality, to have one's misdeeds "recorded" carries enormous weight. The Namahage book does not need to exist in reality; its imagined authority is enough. Children learn that nothing can be hidden, that the eyes of the community, embodied by the demon, see all and write all.

At the end of the night the book is set aside, returned to a shelf or storage. Its pages never carry names beyond the ritual, but the fear it inscribes into memory is indelible. If the knife cuts and the bucket carries, the book exposes. It frightens not by force but by suggestion, making the child believe that the truth has already been written and cannot be erased.

Section 5: The Wand (Ōnusa)

Among the most striking implements sometimes carried by the Namahage is the purification wand, an ōnusa (also called a haraegushi, and colloquially a gohei): a wooden handle bound with zigzag paper streamers (shide), sometimes mixed with strips of cloth. In shrine practice priests wave these wands over people, objects, and doorways to perform harai, the act of cleansing and driving off malign influence. The lightning-shaped shide are visual cues of that power, a portable boundary-marker like the shimenawa ropes on gates and sacred trees. When the same object appears in horned hands, its charge tilts: what ordinarily signals blessing and protection now arrives as an instrument of inspection and judgment. The wand anchors the Namahage in a recognizable ritual vocabulary, straw, paper, rope, wood, so that even a child can feel that something more than theater has entered the room.

The wand is not universal, and its use varies by hamlet and era, but where it appears the effect is immediate. White shide catch and toss the lamplight; their papery whisper adds a counterpoint to straw rasp and boot thump; a single sweep can seem to redraw the air of the room. Children who have seen priests wield the same form at festivals suddenly meet it at their own threshold, and categories collapse: sacred and demonic share a tool. For adults, the wand reads as a visible warrant, a sign that the accusations and bargains of the visit carry more than neighborhood backing. It helps pace the encounter, flourish, pause, pronouncement, and ties the house call to New Year purification without a word being said.

There is a paradox here: how can a demon carry the priest's instrument of purification? Folklorists suggest that this inversion is intentional, demonstrating the thin line between the divine and the demonic in rural imagination. The Namahage is not wholly monster; it is also a messenger, a liminal figure who brings both terror and cleansing. To see the ōnusa in demon hands is to be reminded that fear can purify as effectively as prayer.

For children, the wand is bewildering. They may have seen the same object at shrine festivals, waved by priests in robes, accompanied by solemn chants. To encounter it in their own home, brandished by horned figures demanding obedience, collapses categories. Sacred and profane blur, leaving only the impression that powers larger than the household have intervened. The shide's movement reinforces this impression: its constant flickering seems alive, an extension of the mask's eyes or the knife's blade, yet softer and more pervasive.

Parents interpret the ōnusa as a seal of seriousness. While the knife or bucket may frighten by threat, the wand suggests that the ritual itself carries divine sanction. Promises made in its presence feel binding, as though witnessed not just by neighbors in costume but by forces beyond human control. This strengthens the negotiation phase of the visit, when parents defend their children and agree to improvements. A bow before the ōnusa has the weight of a vow.

Performers, too, find the wand useful. Its lightness allows for dramatic gestures, flourishes, sudden flicks, sweeping motions across the room. Unlike the heavy knife or bucket, it requires little strength, enabling the demon to move with speed and rhythm. The sound of the paper shide, faint but distinctive, adds another layer to the performance, a dry whisper counterpoint to the booming voice and thumping steps. The wand allows the Namahage to control not only fear but atmosphere.

The symbolism resonates with broader Japanese traditions of purification and boundary-setting. The New Year, when the Namahage appear, is itself a liminal time, a passage from old to new. It is the season of cleansing, when households sweep out dust, discard broken tools, and prepare offerings for the Toshigami deities. To bring the ōnusa into the home at this moment underlines the ritual's function: the demons are not only accusers but cleaners, scouring away sloth and disobedience just as priests sweep away impurity.

Children often recall the wand with mixed feelings. Some remembered it as more frightening than the knife, because it seemed to command the very air, leaving nowhere to hide.

Others remembered it as strangely reassuring, a sign that the demons were not purely malevolent but were also performing a necessary task. This duality, the terror and the cleansing, captures the essence of the Namahage's role in the community.

When the night ends, the ōnusa returns to storage, its shide often wrinkled or torn from vigorous shaking. It may later be burned in a shrine fire, as is customary for ritual paper, so that its use does not linger inappropriately into the ordinary year. The knife and bucket are props that can be stored indefinitely, but the wand carries sacred material that demands renewal. This cyclical replacement mirrors the renewal of the ritual itself, ensuring that fear and purification are always fresh.

The ōnusa reminds us that the Namahage are not mere costumed villagers staging a morality play. They stand at the threshold between human and divine, their implements not only borrowed from daily life but also drawn from ritual practice. By shaking the wand, they declare that the authority of their accusations is sanctioned not just by the community but by the cosmos. In this way, the simplest implement, wood and paper, becomes the most profound.

Section 6: Implements in Concert

The Namahage is remembered first for its mask, its horns, its straw bulk. Yet those who have sat in the dark of a farmhouse during the ritual often recall the implements just as vividly. Fear, after all, comes not only from the sight of a face but from the suggestion of action. A mask stares, but a knife can cut. A bucket can carry. A book can expose. A wand can cleanse or condemn. Each tool extends the Namahage beyond mere appearance, giving it reach into body, reputation, and spirit.

Taken separately, the implements speak to different kinds of threat. The knife threatens cutting, symbolically stripping away sloth. The bucket threatens removal, sometimes played as hauling off the child, more often as carrying away the "blisters" of laziness. The book threatens exposure, as if misdeeds were already written down. The wand threatens divine sanction. Their power lies not in execution but in implication.

Together, the implements form a common thread of ritual fear. The knife punctuates with force, the bucket provides a hollow echo, the book supplies authority, the wand overlays sanctity. None of these elements is accidental. They mirror the layers of discipline that shape rural life: physical labor, household obedience, communal reputation, spiritual order. The Namahage does not simply shout these values. It embodies them through objects.

There is also a deep theatrical intelligence in this array. Props anchor performance. They give young men in masks something to do with their hands, something to strike against the floor, something to thrust toward a trembling child. They transform noise into choreography. Without them, the ritual would be shouting in straw. With them, it becomes a complete drama, its symbols clear even to those too young to follow the words.

Implements also ground the ritual in the material world of the village. The knife is carved from local wood, the bucket built from slats in the carpenter's shed, the book borrowed from the schoolhouse, the wand made with paper folded at the shrine. Nothing is exotic. Each item is drawn from the life of the community, then twisted into a new role for one night. This transformation is key. Fear arises not from something alien, but from the ordinary made strange. The child who helps fetch water in the bucket in the morning now sees it as an instrument of abduction at night. The same familiarity that once bred comfort becomes the root of terror.

In this way, implements ensure the Namahage's impact extends beyond the ritual itself. They plant fear in the objects of daily life. A child cannot see the knife in the kitchen, the bucket by the well, the ledger on a shelf, or the wand at a shrine without some faint echo of the demons' visit. The implements carry the memory forward into every day of the year.

For the adults, too, the implements hold meaning. The knife reminds them of discipline, the bucket of the cost of laziness, the book of communal accountability, the wand of sacred order. Each speaks not only to children but to parents, who must uphold the same values in quieter ways once the shouting fades. To pour sake into the bucket or bow before the wand is to reaffirm that the household accepts its place in the fabric of the village.

By the end of the night, the implements return to shelves and storage. They lose their demonic aura and resume their ordinary functions. Yet for those who lived through the ritual, the memory clings. Implements ensure that the Namahage is not confined to masks in the snow but woven into the grain of everyday life. They are the bridge between costume and community, between fear in the moment and discipline that endures.

The Namahage's implements remind us of a truth about ritual: that symbols gain their power not from rarity but from familiarity. A sword pulled from a temple vault might awe for its craftsmanship, but a bucket lifted from beside the hearth terrifies precisely because it is known. Implements prove that fear can live in the ordinary. They show that the strongest rituals do not rely on distance from daily life, but on its transformation.

When the pounding at the door fades and the masks vanish into snow, what remains in the house are not only memories of faces and voices, but impressions of tools, objects that will be seen again tomorrow, drained of terror yet still shadowed by it. The child who grips the bucket handle to fetch water will remember the threat it once carried. The parent who sharpens a kitchen knife will hear in its scrape the echo of accusation. The implements ensure the lesson continues, quietly, year after year.

CHAPTER 7: The Visit: A Night of Fear

Section 1: At the Genkan

The first sound is fists on wood. A dull, flat pounding that makes the lintel quiver and the iron latch rattle in its bracket. The house tightens around it, timbers flexing, paper lanterns trembling on their hooks, a coal in the hibachi breathing a little brighter in the draft. Outside there is the hiss of snow, constant, small, like a thousand soft hands rubbing the night to keep it alive. Inside there is breath, the brief knock of a tea bowl set too hard on the floor, a whispered name. And then the fists again, three thuds in a row, spaced as if to say: *We are here. We are here. We are not patient.*

No one moves at first. The children have already been warned. It is late, and the house is closed against the cold. The front entryway, the genkan, is narrow wooden, built to keep wind from running a straight line from door to hearth. A father sits nearest the door, legs folded, hands on his knees. He has the stillness of someone holding his pulse down by force. The mother's palm is on a child's shoulder, a slow circle to quiet a heart. An older aunt sets chopsticks gently across a bowl and glances at the ceiling as if the roof might answer for them.

The third round of pounding is not fists but an open palm, broad, slapping, making the wood jump. Then comes the scrape of straw against bark, the shuffle and grunt of something heavy adjusting its stance in front of the doorstep, and a low voice from the other side of the door, loud enough to carry through the beam:

「悪い子はいねが！」 *Warui ko wa inē ga!? — Are there any bad children here?*

The father rises, bows toward the closed door out of habit or hope, then lifts the latch. The door resists: snow pressed against it from the outside, weight in the seam. He puts his shoulder to the wood and the line of light opens. Immediately the cold enters, full and wild, pricking the inside of the nostrils, flattening the flame in the oil lamp, raising gooseflesh along exposed wrists. The night smells of smoke, pine, and the ferrous edge of frost. It smells of straw, clean and dusty at the same time, a field carried on shoulders.

They fill the doorway before they step through it, those horned faces with their carved brows and painted mouths. The eyes have been cut so that the whites glare even in weak light. Teeth are clearly visible and catch the lamplight like enamel. The horns vary but add to the imposition. Nothing on these faces is polite. They are built to be larger than a man, to magnify his outline into something that can occupy a family's entire vision. On their shoulders, woven coats of straw (*mino*) hang heavy and wet at the edges, bellies of straw swollen with melted snow that drips in a slow rhythm onto the planks.

They step inside.

The first brush of a sleeve against the doorframe sheds a sheet of straw that patters on the floor like dry rain. The tatami where they stand shows a trail of winter, dark patches, grit from the fields, the faint slur of a footprint dissolving. The lead figure straightens to his full height and the ceiling beam answers with a small groan. His voice is not only his voice; it is a made thing, pushed through the mask and the night until it becomes something else.

「泣ぐ子はいねが！」 *Nagu ko wa inē ga!? — Are there any crying children!?*

The little boy's breath disappears. His mother's hand tightens, firm enough to hurt. Somewhere behind them the aunt murmurs the boy's name with a bit of warning shaped into it, as if a name could be a shield. The second figure stamps once. Snow shakes loose from the fringe of his sleeves and jumps as little white flecks in the lamplight.

「怠け者はいねが！」 *Namake-mono wa inē ga!?* — *Any lazy ones!?*

「親の言うことを聞いでるが！」 *Oya no iu koto o kiideru ga!?* — *Do you obey your parents!?*

The father bows again, lower, and begins to speak in a voice that even he does not recognize as his, soft, bargaining, proud and ashamed at once. He says the children are good. He says they have studied. He says that the boy has been more obedient with his mother and that the girl learned three new kanji and that both of them have promised to be better in the new year. He says this because he believes it and because belief has nothing to do with what the night demands.

From inside the straw sleeve, the lead figure produces a book. Its cover is dark, swollen at the edges from years of snow and smoke. The pages are thick and irregular, some corners folded, others stained. When he opens it, the paper whispers against itself.

He drags a finger down a column, pauses, then grunts. His voice, muffled by the mask, carries the sound of reading even if no one can see the characters.

「怠けて薪を運ばなかった子は誰だ…」
Who was it that shirked carrying firewood…

The boy stiffens. That was yesterday's chore. No one outside the family could have known. The father bows lower, words tumbling: the boy did help, he insists, he only grew tired at the end. The demon turns another page slowly, as if unconvinced, as if more faults are written there waiting their turn.

To the children, the book is unbearable proof: the Namahage have been watching, recording, remembering. The night is no longer just a performance. It is judgment, and judgment has ink.

The lead mask turns its blank eyes toward the boy. The carved pupils are black, and yet whatever sees within sees accurately. The voice drops lower, intimate somehow under the roar: 「嘘ついてねが？」 *Uso tsuitenega?* — *You're not lying, are you?* The boy's lips part without sound. His face has that wet shine a child's face gets when tears climb before they fall. He nods, then remembers not to nod, and shakes his head instead. The demon breathes out hard enough to flicker the lamp.

The mother tries to lift her chin and fails. She manages words, bows, apologizes for anything they have done or left undone, thanks the Namahage for their trouble, as if trouble were a parcel carried across town. The aunt stands now too, hands folded in front of her, and says that the children have been very good this year, actually, but their goodness will be even better after tonight.

The father offers sake, small cups on a tray, both hands extended. The lead mask accepts with a gesture that manages to be not human and yet precise. It is a theatrical motion, and the children are meant to see it. The cup disappears into a black slit of mouth where no mouth is, and then comes back empty, and this impossibility becomes true because it must be. The aunt refills. The younger cousin takes his cup and pretends the mask cannot find his lips; the older demon cuffs him lightly behind the head, a flick that makes the straw rustle like laughter. The parents pretend not to notice.

Now the questions sharpen. They use names. The boy is accused of leaving chores unfinished, of ignoring tasks set by his parents. The girl is reprimanded for neglecting her studies, for failing to complete her homework when diligence was expected. The voices drop to a growl, then rise again into the same commands every family in the village has heard for generations:

「怠けるな！」 *Namakeru na!* — *Do not be lazy!*

「勉強しろ！」 *Benkyō shiro!* — *Study!*

「親の言うことを聞け！」 *Oya no iu koto o kike!* — *Listen to your parents!*

The boy lets two tears slide free, then swallows the rest. His sister bites the inside of her cheek, her gaze fixed on the floorboards. She has learned to believe that looking down will shield her, that if she refuses eye contact the demons will not see her thoughts. It is a child's logic, thin as paper. The straw brushes her shoulder as one figure leans close, and the sound is enough to undo the illusion: the hiss of field grass in a place where no field belongs, the raw scrape of outdoors pulled into the house. She gasps. Not from pain, but from the unbearable wrongness of it.

In the corner, the smallest dog does not bark. He has no bark left in him. His ears flatten against his skull, and his body lowers until he seems to melt into the floorboards. The larger dog has long since hidden itself under the overhang outside; its silence is proof of a different kind of wisdom. Only the cat has vanished completely, having found the gap behind a chest and slipped into the darkness.

The room is filled with sound already. It is not only voices. Every gesture carries weight: the crunch of straw sleeves rubbing together, the drip of melted snow hitting tatami, the hollow creak of wood under unfamiliar weight. The demons do not hurry. Their stillness is as deliberate as their noise. They let silence stretch, force it to bind the family in place. Every breath grows louder, every heartbeat sharper, until the smallest shift in posture feels like a confession.

The father bows lower than he has yet, his hands pressed to his thighs, his forehead dipping close to the mat. He speaks with a voice that belongs not to a man but to the line of men before him, the rehearsed humility of son and grandson echoing inside his chest. He says they will do better. He says the boy will rise earlier to split kindling without complaint, that the girl will study harder, not just enough to pass, but enough to earn her teacher's praise. He says the family as a whole will be less sharp with one another, more obedient, more diligent. His words fall in measured cadence, like items being set upon a table, one by one, to see if the offering will satisfy.

The demons do not answer at once. They tilt their masks by degrees, letting the carved eyes dwell on the children, letting the straw drip onto the floor like grains of an hourglass. Time itself is part of the test. At last, one figure exhales through the slit of his mask, a slow, heavy breath that makes the oil lamp stutter. It is not approval, nor forgiveness. It is acknowledgment. Judgment rendered not with words but with the weight of waiting. The family bows deeper still, repeating their promises, as if repetition could nail them in place.

The boy cannot hold still any longer. His hands twitch on his knees, and one betrays him by rising toward his face to wipe a tear. The demon's head snaps, following the motion, and the boy freezes, hand suspended. For an instant the whole room tilts toward him. Then, mercifully, the mask turns away again. The boy drops his hand as though it has been burned and presses it hard against his thigh. He learns, in that instant, what every child of Oga has learned: tears are not enough to end the questioning. Only promises, and the adults who make them, can draw the night toward its close.

The mother speaks now. Her voice is low but steady, a current that runs beneath the roar. She thanks the visitors for their trouble, bows with careful dignity, and assures them that their words have taken root. She does not protest innocence. She does not beg. She frames the family's faults as a field in need of tending, and the demons as the plow. She knows, as her own mother knew, that resistance is useless. She offers gratitude instead, turning judgment into blessing by the act of saying so.

The second demon shifts his stance, stamping once. Snow loosens from his sleeves and scatters across the mat. He points, to the children. His voice drops into a formal register, as if pronouncing something more than scolding:

「怠け心、落としていけ。」
Namake-gokoro, otoshite ike.
Let go of the lazy heart.

The children stare back at the masks. The message is not only for them; it is for the house itself. Laziness must be left behind like an impurity, shed like straw at the threshold.

The ritual has reached its balance point. The demons have demanded, the family has promised. Fear has done its work. Now comes the unwinding, slow and deliberate. The lead mask tips his head, a gesture small enough to seem accidental and large enough to feel like release. He shifts a foot backward toward the threshold. The air in the room eases. Shoulders drop, lungs expand. The rope of silence that had bound them begins to loosen, strand by strand.

But the departure is never sudden. One final moment must stretch, a reminder that the visit is not a game. The demon pauses in the doorway, half inside, half out, horns framed against the lintel's shadow. Snow swirls past his back in thin, silver flakes. He does not speak yet. He looks. He looks at the boy whose tears still cling to his lashes. He looks at the girl who has made herself small against her mother's side. He looks at the father, bent and stiff, and at the mother, who holds the weight of the household in her bow. In that silence sits everything: the end of the year, the ache of hunger in a winter village, the pride of young men who shout at their elders for one night and then resume their roles, the memory the children will keep for years.

Then the mask speaks, quieter now, so the children must strain to hear:

「怠け心を捨てろ。」

Namake-gokoro o sutero.

Throw away the lazy heart.

And then louder, so the beams and roof itself must carry it:

「また来るぞ！」

Mata kuru zo!

We will come again!

The words are a promise and a threat, both.

They step back into the night. The door closes with the weight of wood meeting wood, the latch finding its place by instinct. Cold air curls inside for a last instant, then withdraws. Already the snow begins to erase the tracks on the threshold, lifting edges, blurring heels, softening prints until they look less like signs of passage and more like fragments of a dream. Inside, the lamp steadies, its flame no longer flattened.

The mother's hand leaves the boy's shoulder. It comes away damp, warm with the heat of fear. The aunt bends and gathers fallen straw one stalk at a time, as though the remnants were precious, or dangerous, or both. She places them in a neat pile beside the hearth, where they will burn tomorrow with the smell of wet field grass.

For a minute, no one speaks. The silence now is different: not heavy, not binding, but tentative, like the hush that follows a storm when the wind has gone but the trees still remember shaking. The children breathe in short, careful pulls, the kind that hope not to be noticed. The brazier hisses as a drop of spilled sake meets its rim. The room warms again. Details sharpen. Meltwater traces dark maps across the floorboards.

Outside, the night goes on. Voices echo in other lanes, laughter and cries carried thin on the wind. The Namahage are at another door, or perhaps already leaving it. They are both singular and countless, both these two men and all the men who ever wore the mask.

The father remains kneeling for a long time. He glances at his son. The boy meets his gaze, eyes shining with water, but steady now.

"Tomorrow," the father says, his voice his own again, "we will carry wood together."

The boy nods, quick, certain, as though nodding itself might make him stronger. The girl wipes her nose on her sleeve and sits straighter, trying to shape herself into diligence before the morning comes. The mother exhales, long and slow.

Much later, the children will sleep, curled into the warmth fear has left behind, the hollow it carved still warm like the nest of a great animal. The adults will whisper across the room. The lamp will dim to ember, ember to ash, ash to grey dust. Dawn will paint a thin gloss of frost across the world.

But for now the door is closed, the masks are gone.

「また来るぞ。」

Mata kuru zo.

We will come again.

Section 2: Ritual Mechanics: Controlled Chaos

The pounding and shouting may feel wild, but nothing about the Namahage visit is random. Beneath the terror lies a choreography that the community has practiced for centuries.

To the children it is chaos; to the adults, it is discipline enacted through theater.

The men inside the masks are typically the younger members of the village, unmarried men, apprentices, cousins not yet burdened with their own children. They have energy to spare, and the ritual demands it. On this night they are allowed to overturn their own identities and become something larger, louder, more terrifying. The straw transforms them: hands become claws, shoulders become mountains, their voices, distorted through wood and echo, become the roar of something ancient.

Each household knows they are coming. This is not an ambush but a summons. The door is not broken down; it is opened. Parents pretend reluctance, but they have already prepared sake, already explained to the children why tonight will be different. In some homes, mothers whisper warnings weeks in advance: *Study harder, or the Namahage will know.* Fathers sharpen their tone at the table: *Don't be lazy, remember who visits in December.* The ritual begins long before the pounding on the door.

When the Namahage step inside, the first act is accusation: laziness, disobedience, lying. The accusations are always phrased as questions, not statements. 「怠け者はいねが！」 *Namake-mono wa inē ga!?* — *Any lazy ones here!?* The question form is deliberate. A statement can be denied, but a question demands an answer, even if that answer is silence. Silence itself becomes guilt.

The second act is negotiation. Parents defend their children, justify their behavior, promise improvement. This, too, is expected. A household that did not speak in defense of its children would be shamed as negligent. The louder the demons shout, the more earnestly the parents respond. In this clash, demon accusation against parental defense, the children sit at the center, feeling the weight of both sides.

The third act is instruction. Once the resistance has been tested, the Namahage issue direct commands:

「勉強しろ！」　*Benkyō shiro!* — *Study harder!*

「親に逆らうな！」　*Oya ni sakarau na!* — *Don't defy your parents!*

These imperatives cut through the noise with blunt force. Children hear them not from their parents, whose voices can be ignored, but from something beyond the family, something larger than the household walls.

Finally comes the release. Promises are made, often out loud, sometimes repeated word for word after the demons. Parents pour sake, bow, and thank the Namahage for their trouble. The demons accept this gratitude as if they were gods receiving offerings. And then, just as suddenly as they arrived, they leave, straw brushing wood, voices fading into the snow.

Every step is ritualized, yet within those steps is space for improvisation. A demon may focus on a particular child, pressing harder than expected. A parent may defend more fiercely, turning the exchange into a kind of theater that the neighbors gossip about for weeks. But no matter the variation, the bones of the ritual remain the same: accusation, negotiation, instruction, release.

To the children, it is terror. To the parents, it is reinforcement. To the community, it is continuity, the same script performed year after year, generation after generation, proving that the line between chaos and order is thin but deliberate.

Section 3: Reflection

When the Namahage leave and the door shuts, silence falls. The straw is swept, the sake cups rinsed, the fire coaxed back into warmth. On the surface, life returns to normal. Yet the ritual lingers, an echo in the body, a memory in the mind, a weight in the community. The true work of the Namahage is not in the pounding fists or the shouted questions, but in what remains afterward.

For the children, the visit is unforgettable. It marks them with fear, yes, but also with belonging. The terror is specific: the mask's blank eyes, the straw's rasp on skin, the voice booming their name. No lecture from a parent could have this effect. It is one thing to be scolded at the table; it is another to have the very air of the room bend around a horned figure demanding obedience.

And yet the fear is not permanent trauma. Children grow into adults who laugh about their terror, but never forget it. In interviews decades later, men and women from Oga will still recall their Namahage nights with remarkable clarity: the pounding, the roaring, the promises made in tears. The ritual plants a memory so deep that even when fear softens, accountability remains.

Psychologists might call it *ritualized stress inoculation*. To face fear in a controlled setting builds resilience. But for the villagers, it was simpler: the Namahage taught children that laziness and disobedience had consequences, not abstract ones, but embodied and immediate. The demons were real for that night, and so too was the lesson.

The parents, too, are implicated. The Namahage's questions are aimed not only at children but at the family unit. If a child has been lazy, who allowed it? If a child disobeys, who failed to correct them? In defending their children, parents rehearse their own responsibilities. They cannot shrug off the accusations; to do so would be to admit weakness, negligence, failure of duty.

There is shame in the performance, but it is productive shame. The parents bow, negotiate, promise. In doing so, they publicly reassert their role as guardians and teachers. The Namahage remind them: you are accountable not just to your household, but to the village.

In Japan, where silence and indirectness often govern communication, the Namahage break through that quiet. They give voice to what is usually left unsaid: that families owe diligence, that idleness is contagious, that discipline is communal. The shouts may be frightening, but they are also clarifying. They allow truths to be spoken aloud without direct blame between neighbors.

The Namahage visit every house. No one is exempt. The mayor's child and the fisherman's child tremble under the same mask, and in that way the ritual becomes for the community as a whole, not only for individuals. It creates a shared experience of accountability, binding the village in a single rhythm: every door pounded, every child accused, every promise extracted.

This universality is key. If only some families received visits, shame would isolate them. By making the ritual communal, shame becomes shared, and thus bearable. The demons shout at everyone, so no one can say they alone were singled out. This levels the hierarchy, at least for one night.

The ritual also ties the living to the dead. The Namahage echo ancestors' voices, enforcing the rules that kept generations alive through famine, storm, and winter. To bow to the demon is to bow to continuity. To endure the visit is to prove one's place in the unbroken line of survival.

In fear lies the paradox. Often thought destructive, here it becomes a teacher. The difference is control. Ritual fear is bounded, cyclical, expected. The Namahage come once a year, on schedule, with rules. They roar, they accuse, they command, but then they leave. Children are left shaken but safe, taught but not broken.

This controlled fear channels chaos into meaning. It is not the random terror of a storm or the cruelty of an abuser. It is structured, communal, and purifying. Fear, in this form, disciplines without destroying.

The anthropologist Clifford Geertz once wrote that rituals are "models of" and "models for" reality: they both represent the world and instruct people how to live in it. The Namahage are precisely this. They represent the dangers of idleness, disobedience, and neglect. And they model the correction: confession, promise, renewal.

Western observers often compare Japan to "guilt cultures" like those shaped by Christianity, where morality is internalized and sin is between the individual and God. Japan, by contrast, is frequently described as a "shame culture," where morality is enforced externally, through community and reputation. The Namahage embody this distinction. They are shame made flesh: the eyes of the village in horned masks, the voice of accountability booming into your home.

This is not to say one system is better than the other, but it shows how deeply culture shapes morality. In a land of close-knit villages and harsh winters, survival depended on conformity and discipline. Shame, performed collectively through rituals like the Namahage, was the most effective glue.

As we saw earlier in the masks and garb, horned figures haunt festivals across Europe. But their purpose is not only spectacle. Like the Namahage, they discipline through fear: Krampus chasing children into obedience, Mamuthones clattering their bells as warnings, Kukeri purging laziness with noise and chaos. Across cultures, the form differs, but the function is shared: fear turned into memory, chaos into lesson.

All of these rituals share the same DNA: terror contained by tradition, fear wielded as discipline. Humanity, it seems, has always known that reason alone is not enough. Children, and perhaps adults, need to feel fear in their bones to remember the weight of responsibility.

The Namahage, then, are not just local folklore. They are one expression of a universal human truth: that fear, when ritualized, becomes a kind of moral pedagogy. It is not fear for its own sake, but fear transformed into lesson, into memory, into continuity.

The pounding stops, the masks leave, the door shuts. But the ritual is not over. Its work continues in the silence afterward, in the child who sits a little straighter the next day, in the parent who speaks more firmly, in the village that breathes easier knowing discipline has been reaffirmed.

The Namahage are terrifying, yes. But they are also necessary. Without them, winter might still crush the fields, but worse, it might also creep into the hearts of children, softening them into complacency. With them, the village remembers that survival demands vigilance, effort, and obedience to the collective.

Fear is not the opposite of love in this ritual. It is its companion. The demons roar not because they hate, but because they must remind the living how to endure.

Section 4: The Silence After

The door is closed now. The latch has settled into its groove, and the wind rattles only the outer shutters, not the bones of the house. The straw scattered across the tatami has been swept into a corner pile, a few strands still clinging stubbornly to the weave. The fire burns low, coals glowing like watchful eyes.

The children have gone quiet at last. They breathe in the shallow rhythm of exhaustion, cheeks still damp, bodies curled tight against their mother. Their dreams will be restless, but they will sleep. The father sits in silence, hands resting on his knees, staring at the door as if the masks might press their faces against it once more. The aunt hums under her breath while she feeds the last straw into the brazier, and it hisses into smoke, filling the air with the smell of field and frost.

Outside, snow falls without pause. The lane is already softening, the sharp edges of the demons' footprints blurring, filling, erasing. By morning, no trace will remain except what was left inside. The questions, however, do not melt. They sit in the beams and in the rafters, echoing under the skin.

The fire crackles. The house exhales. The year turns.

And somewhere, beyond the snow-covered fields, the Namahage walk on, leaving silence in their wake, carrying with them the ancient burden of reminding the living that nothing is free, not even tomorrow.

CHAPTER 8: The Necessity of Fear

Section 1: Fear as a Human Constant

Fear is among the oldest and most durable of human companions. Long before ritual, before language itself, there was the jolt of recognition that something threatened survival. Evolution wired it into the nervous system: the quickening of pulse, the tightening of muscles, the dilation of pupils. A sudden sound in the brush, a shadow that moves too fast, the sensation of being watched, all provoke responses that operate faster than thought. Flight, fight, or freezing in place, these instincts secured the survival of fragile creatures who lacked claws, armor, or speed. In this sense, fear is not an intrusion on human life but one of its conditions.

Every culture has wrestled with the problem of what to do with this force. If left unshaped, fear can fracture communities, leaving people paralyzed or suspicious of one another. It can harden into trauma, preventing memory from settling into usable knowledge. It can be exploited by tyrants who cultivate perpetual dread. But fear can also be harnessed. One of the distinguishing features of human societies is their ability to take raw impulses and convert them into patterned, repeatable forms. As hunger found form in cuisine and sexuality in kinship, so fear found its form in ritual, patterned, disciplined, and communal.

Anthropologists have long noted that across the globe, rituals of fear appear at critical thresholds: coming of age, entry into adulthood, seasonal changes, or times of environmental danger. The scarification rites of parts of Africa, the initiation seclusions of Melanesia, the masked dances of the American Southwest, all employ elements of fright, disorientation, or endurance. Their purpose is rarely to harm. Instead they transform an uncontrollable emotion into a structured passage. By frightening together, societies ensure that individuals learn the difference between private panic and collective trial.

The anthropologist Victor Turner called such moments "liminal," standing between one state and another. Fear plays a central role in liminality because it strips away ordinary bearings. The youth in initiation faces masked figures whose identity is concealed; the initiate into a mystery cult enters a darkened chamber; the child in Oga sees horns in the doorway and realizes the home is not entirely safe. Fear destabilizes, but in ritual it destabilizes with purpose. It forces a confrontation with vulnerability, a reminder that safety is not natural but constructed by the community.

From a psychological perspective, the universality of fear rituals makes sense. The human brain is wired to learn most deeply when aroused by strong emotion. A sudden jolt sears the lesson into memory, much as a burn teaches caution faster than any verbal warning. Communities discovered, long before neuroscience could explain it, that fear educates with unusual efficiency. A single terrifying night can anchor a lesson that parents or teachers struggle to instill through months of gentle instruction.

The Namahage are one instance of this broader pattern, extending the comparisons glimpsed earlier in their masks and performances. But here the point is broader still: ritualized fear is not Japanese alone, but human. European children met Krampus or Perchten in Alpine villages, their horns and chains echoing through snowy streets. Sardinia's Mamuthones moved through towns in heavy black masks, weighed down with cowbells that thundered with each step. In the Caribbean, Junkanoo processions once terrified as well as delighted, with costumed figures chasing children through alleys. In each case, communities found it effective to embody fear in a tangible figure, something that entered the streets or homes, visible and undeniable, too large to be ignored.

Fear thus appears not as an accidental by-product of culture but as one of its building blocks. Communities ritualize it because they must: survival requires vigilance, memory requires markers, morality requires external reminders. In this sense, fear is not opposed to community but foundational to it. To gather in winter darkness and face down a masked visitor is to reaffirm that one is part of a group strong enough to endure. The visitor's terror is proof of solidarity, the ordeal a rehearsal for the harsher ordeals that climate or scarcity will bring.

The challenge, of course, is to strike balance. Raw fear corrodes; it divides rather than unites. If the terror is too overwhelming, children fall ill or families refuse participation. If it is too weak, the lesson evaporates. The genius of ritualized fear lies in its calibration. It is repeated often enough to be expected, limited in duration so that relief follows closely on panic, and framed by communal recognition that what has happened is for the good. It is terror under license, dread domesticated for instruction.

To say that humans need fear is not to say they need suffering for its own sake. Rather, they need occasions where the inevitability of danger is acknowledged and rehearsed. In a world where illness, famine, flood, or fire could appear without warning, it made sense to prepare children with controlled shocks. The Namahage's accusations rehearse this logic. Better to cry under the straw gaze of a neighbor than to falter unprepared when real misfortune arrives. The rite trains endurance in advance of necessity.

In this light, the Namahage join a long lineage of figures who make fear collective rather than private. They remind us that the pulse of terror, the trembling in the gut, is not only a biological reflex but also a cultural resource. By channeling fear into ritual, communities take what is otherwise destabilizing and make it formative. They prove that even the most primal emotions can be given shape, and that in that shape lies both memory and belonging.

Section 2: The Shape of Ritual Fear

If fear is a human constant, ritual fear is its refinement. Across cultures, societies have learned to distinguish between the chaos of raw panic and the structured shock of a controlled ordeal. The difference is not trivial. Raw fear arrives unannounced, triggered by accident or attack. Ritual fear is summoned deliberately, prepared and bounded by form. What makes ritual fear so effective is that it takes an ungovernable impulse and places it within limits, creating a pattern that can be repeated without collapsing into cruelty.

Several features mark this transformation. The first is predictability. Rituals of fear occur at known times, often tied to the calendar. In Oga, children know that the last night of December will bring the Namahage. The approach of winter, the rhythm of the year, makes their visit inevitable. This foreknowledge alters the quality of the encounter. Unlike a sudden accident, which leaves the body in stunned disarray, ritual fear is anticipated. Anticipation itself heightens anxiety, but also prepares the ground for meaning. Children may dread the knock at the door, but in dreading they are already participating in the ritual's lesson: one must be ready for trials that arrive with the seasons.

The second feature is containment. Ritual fear is not permitted to spill without end. The Namahage enter, accuse, chase, and depart. The ordeal lasts minutes, not days. Once the door closes behind them, the household breathes again, laughter breaks the tension, and ordinary life resumes. This containment makes the fear bearable. It ensures that the terror does not metastasize into trauma. The structure of beginning, climax, and release gives participants a narrative shape, transforming what could be chaos into story. Fear without boundaries corrodes; fear with boundaries educates.

The third feature is authority. Those who embody fear in ritual are sanctioned by the community. The men who wear horns and straw in Oga are neighbors, fathers, uncles. They are recognized, at least by adults, as legitimate agents of the tradition. This authority distinguishes ritual fear from cruelty. A bully who terrifies for amusement has no sanction, no broader frame to justify his act. A Namahage, by contrast, terrifies as a delegate of the community. The mask is both disguise and authorization. When the demon raises his voice, he does so not as an individual but as the embodiment of collective will.

The final feature is the aftermath. Ritual fear does not end in isolation but in relief and often in laughter. The Namahage departs, the child wipes away tears, the parents pour sake for the performers. The community reasserts its cohesion. What lingers is not the raw panic of an accident but the sharpened memory of a shared event. The rhythm of fear and relief is crucial. It teaches that ordeals can be endured, that fear can pass, and that community persists.

When seen together, these features, predictability, containment, authority, aftermath, form the skeleton of ritual fear. They transform an experience that might otherwise fragment into something that can be repeated, remembered, and cherished.

The Namahage are a striking example, but the pattern holds elsewhere. As we noted earlier, Alpine winter traditions feature horned figures who appear on the same December nights each year; their rampages, though noisy, are limited to an evening; their authority derives from custom and village sanction; and their departure is followed by feasting. Even haunted houses in contemporary amusement parks echo this shape. Visitors anticipate their terror, enter controlled spaces, trust in the authority of staff and designers, and emerge laughing. The persistence of this structure suggests that it meets deep psychological and social needs.

What is distinctive about ritual fear is that it allows societies to cultivate vulnerability without destruction. To frighten children outside any frame would be abuse; to frighten them within the ritual's boundaries becomes instruction. The difference lies not in the intensity of the emotion but in the architecture around it. That architecture makes the experience legible, shared, and therefore safe to remember. It converts panic into pedagogy.

It is this shaping that explains why figures like the Namahage endure. Without form, the shock of a horned figure in the doorway would dissipate into cruelty or chaos. With form, it becomes a durable tradition that can be repeated for centuries. The shape of ritual fear is its guarantee of survival. So long as the visit can be anticipated, contained, authorized, and resolved, the demons at the door can continue to terrify without destroying.

Section 3: Fear, Discipline, and Moral Education

If ritual fear differs from raw fear by its structure, its purpose lies in the lessons it delivers. Communities do not frighten their children merely to produce screams. They frighten them to shape behavior, to drive home responsibilities that might otherwise fade into neglect. The Namahage's entrance each New Year is framed by questions, and those questions expose the moral core of the ritual. "Have you been lazy? Have you helped your parents? Have you studied?" These are not arbitrary terrors but focused interrogations, aimed at the failings that most concerned a community struggling against winter scarcity. Fear becomes the medium of discipline.

The effectiveness of this pedagogy rests on immediacy. A scolding voice from a parent can be deflected, excused, or ignored. A demon in the doorway, horns gleaming and straw brushing the walls, cannot be dismissed so easily. The lesson is embodied. Children see their shortcomings made visible, called out by a figure that seems larger than human. The suddenness of the encounter leaves little room for rationalization. For many who recall their childhood visits, the shame of being named lingers longer than the fear itself. The Namahage teaches not by abstract principle but by dramatized exposure.

Other cultures have recognized the same principle, though they have framed it differently. In European Christendom, fear was used from pulpits to enforce moral discipline. Hellfire sermons painted vivid images of eternal torment, meant to jolt the conscience into repentance. The logic was parallel: frighten in order to correct. Yet there is a critical difference. The preacher's hell was invisible, deferred to an afterlife. The Namahage's terror was immediate and physical, enacted in the home. One threatened abstract punishment, the other delivered embodied confrontation.

A gentler counterpart can be found in the figure of Santa Claus. The promise that only obedient children receive gifts is, at root, a discipline of fear: fear of exclusion, fear of disappointment. But Santa's fear is softened, cushioned by generosity. The Namahage, by contrast, arrives with menace first, blessing second. Where Santa withholds, Namahage accuses. Both rituals discipline, but they do so in different registers, one by offering reward, the other by dramatizing punishment.

This distinction underscores a larger point. Fear-based discipline does not need to be cruel to be effective, but it does need to be credible. Children must believe that their actions have consequences, and belief is easier to cultivate when consequences are made tangible. The Namahage achieve this credibility precisely because they enter the household, make eye contact, seize wrists, and demand answers. The performance allows no retreat into abstraction. The child's own conduct is thrust into the center of the room, witnessed by parents, siblings, and neighbors.

The social dimension is crucial. Discipline delivered privately can be evaded or forgotten. Discipline delivered in public, under the gaze of kin and community, sears itself more deeply. The Namahage enforce accountability not only between parent and child but among families as a whole. Each visit confirms that others, too, are being tested. In this way, the ritual transforms private failings into communal concern, binding households into a shared moral order. To see one's neighbor's child weep is to be reminded of one's own duties.

This moral instruction is sharpened by the paradoxical authority of the mask. Everyone knows, at some level, that the demon is a neighbor. But in the moment of the encounter, that knowledge recedes. The mask suspends familiarity, allowing the words spoken behind it to carry unusual weight. When the Namahage accuses a child of sloth, it is not merely an uncle's opinion but the voice of the community embodied. The mask thus enables speech that ordinary social conventions would prohibit. Parents can criticize their children more directly by lending their voice to the demon's mouth.

Over time, the memory of such discipline often transforms into pride. Adults recall their childhood terrors as formative, even humorous. Yet the pride does not erase the original sting. On the contrary, it depends on it. Without the jolt of fear, the lesson would have been forgettable. The transformation of terror into pride is itself a testimony to the effectiveness of the ritual. Fear makes the lesson unforgettable, while the community's framing turns it into a badge of survival.

The Namahage demonstrate a broader truth: fear, when ritualized, can be a powerful instrument of moral education. It can engrave lessons in ways that gentle instruction cannot, precisely because it disrupts the ordinary. But it succeeds only when calibrated, too harsh and it scars, too mild and it trivializes. The balance struck in Oga reflects centuries of refinement, a communal sense of how much fear is enough to correct without destroying.

In this balance lies the genius of the practice. The Namahage do not terrorize indiscriminately. They ask pointed questions, framed by the moral priorities of their society. Their discipline is selective, targeted, and temporary. The lesson is not that life is hopelessly fearful, but that effort and responsibility are non-negotiable. The terror is a means, not an end. It exists to remind children and parents alike that survival depends on diligence, and that negligence has consequences.

Thus, the Namahage illustrate how fear, far from being a primitive residue, can be shaped into a pedagogy of responsibility. Communities across the world have relied on similar devices, but the Oga practice highlights the power of embodiment. It is one thing to imagine judgment; it is another to face it in the doorway. The Namahage's gift is to make discipline tangible, to translate abstract duty into a presence that cannot be ignored. In this sense, their frightening visit is not cruelty but instruction, terror transformed into moral education.

Section 4: Psychological Functions of Ritual Fear

If ritualized fear works as moral pedagogy, it does so not only because of the content of its lessons but because of the way fear operates on the mind and body. Psychology provides a second layer of explanation for why such practices endure. Fear is among the most intense human emotions, and intense emotions have distinctive effects: they mark memory, they bond people together, they purge tension, and they elevate ordinary experience into something felt as larger than life. The Namahage ritual exemplifies all of these dynamics.

One of the clearest functions is catharsis. Fear floods the body with adrenaline. Muscles tense, breath shortens, perception sharpens. But when the cause of fear departs, the tension dissolves into relief. The release can bring laughter, sometimes even exhilaration. Children sob as the Namahage demand answers, but minutes later they giggle, the danger already receding. Adults, too, recall the moments of fear as part of a cycle that ended in comfort, warm food, family closeness, reassurance that the ordeal was over. This cathartic release transforms terror into renewal. It is not unlike the relief people seek from horror films or roller coasters: the thrill lies in experiencing fear within a safe frame, followed by the pleasure of release.

A second function is memory marking. Psychological research shows that events experienced under high emotional arousal are encoded more strongly in memory. A dull lecture may fade, but a startling shock lingers. In Oga, countless adults testify to this principle. They can describe the particular mask that visited them decades earlier, the exact words shouted, even the smell of straw in a dark room. The lesson carried by the

Namahage, do not be lazy, be obedient, help your parents, stuck not because it was repeated endlessly but because it was attached to an unforgettable moment of fright. Fear inscribes itself where ordinary admonition fades.

Closely related is the role of bonding. Experiences of fear, when shared, create solidarity. Anthropologists studying initiation rites have long observed that the ordeal binds cohorts together. Those who are frightened together remember the trial as a common passage. In Oga, the scale is smaller but no less real. A child hides behind her mother as the demon enters, only to find her siblings equally terrified. Parents exchange glances as the Namahage delivers his accusations, tacitly acknowledging their own role in upholding discipline. After the departure, neighbors may share laughter, comparing which child cried the loudest. In each case, the emotion that could have isolated becomes a thread of connection. Fear endured together becomes a source of cohesion.

Another function is the production of awe. Fear and awe are closely related states; both involve a sense of being overwhelmed by something larger than oneself. In ritual contexts, this overlap is deliberate. The Namahage are not merely frightening; they are impressive. Their horns, straw cloaks, booming voices, and sudden intrusion create a spectacle that dwarfs ordinary domestic life. For children, this can produce the paradoxical mixture of terror and reverence. They are scared, yet they also feel that they have brushed against something extraordinary. Adults recalling their childhood encounters often describe not only panic but also wonder, the sense that for a moment the ordinary order of things was suspended and a force beyond the everyday entered the room. Awe turns fear into an intimation of the sacred.

These psychological functions are not unique to the Namahage, nor even to ritual. They appear in secular entertainments: haunted houses, ghost stories, horror films, thrill rides. All provide controlled doses of fear, with catharsis, memory, bonding, and awe as the payoff. But what distinguishes the ritual context is the added dimension of moral instruction. Unlike a roller coaster, which frightens for pleasure, the Namahage frighten for discipline. Yet the psychological mechanics are similar, suggesting that humans seek out fear precisely because of the way it sharpens experience and heightens connection.

This helps explain why traditions of ritual fear survive even when belief fades. A child may no longer believe that the Namahage are genuine demons, but the body still reacts, the heart still races, the memory still forms. Parents may invite the visit less for its theological implications than for its psychological efficacy. Outsiders may attend the Sedo Festival and find in it the same thrill they pursue in other spectacles. In each case, the ritual persists because fear continues to work on the body and mind in ways that are both reliable and rewarding.

The Namahage thus illustrate not only a cultural strategy but also a psychological truth: humans benefit from structured experiences of fear. These experiences purge tension, anchor memory, create bonds, and evoke awe. They transform the inevitability of dread into something usable. By staging fear in a way that ends with laughter, memory, solidarity, and wonder, the ritual gives participants a safe encounter with one of life's most destabilizing emotions.

The psychology of fear, far from undermining the ritual, explains its endurance.

Section 5: Fear in Harsh Landscapes

If fear has universal psychological functions, its ritual deployment in Oga and other parts of Japan also reflects a more concrete reality: the demands of environment. Rituals of fear do not arise in a vacuum. They take shape in landscapes that pose particular threats, and they translate those threats into symbolic drama. The snowbound villages of Akita, the fire-prone wooden towns of Yamagata, the typhoon-swept islands of Okinawa each generated rituals that embodied the dangers most pressing to their survival. Fear in these contexts is not only a matter of psychology but of ecology. It is a tool for impressing upon a community the vigilance required by its surroundings.

On the Oga Peninsula, winter was long, isolating, and often brutal. Fishing boats lay idle under heavy snow, fields lay frozen, and the temptation to fall into idleness was real. In such conditions, laziness was not a minor failing but a direct risk to survival. Food stores had to be managed, houses kept warm, tools repaired, nets mended. A family that neglected its tasks could find itself in real peril before the thaw. The Namahage's accusations—"Have you been lazy? Have you worked?"—were not rhetorical. They were a dramatization of the stakes of negligence in an unforgiving climate. The figure of the demon, with its booming voice and sudden entrance, condensed into a single shocking image the truth that complacency in winter could be deadly.

Contrast this with the Kasedori of Yamagata, straw birds who appeared in February. Their ritual was not focused on idleness but on fire prevention. Wooden houses clustered tightly together, their hearths blazing in the cold. One stray spark could destroy an entire village. The Kasedori's straw costumes, drenched with water as they paraded, embodied the threat and the protection simultaneously. Fear here was oriented toward vigilance against flames. The lesson was tailored to the environment: attend to fire, or disaster will follow.

Still further south, the Paantu of Miyako Island smeared mud on houses and bodies. Their purpose was purification, the warding off of misfortune and disease in a subtropical environment where typhoons, pests, and epidemics regularly disrupted life. The fear was less about laziness or fire than about invisible corruption. The Paantu's messy intrusion into the village embodied the principle that impurity must be faced directly and wiped away. Again, the ritual condensed environmental threats into a shocking but manageable encounter.

These examples underline the adaptability of ritual fear. The form, the intrusion of strange figures, the pursuit of children, the disruption of the ordinary, is constant. But the content shifts with ecology. Snow demands diligence, fire demands vigilance, fertility demands purification. Fear is the common medium, but its lesson is inflected by local necessity. This adaptability explains both the ubiquity and the variation of such rituals across Japan and beyond.

For the people of Oga, the harshness of the northern landscape lent particular intensity to the Namahage. Snow did more than inconvenience; it cut villages off, tested their stores, and pressed the community against the edge of endurance. In such an environment, moral discipline was not optional but essential. The ritual served as an annual rehearsal of this fact, imprinting upon children and adults alike the urgency of effort. The figure at the door embodied not only moral authority but also the very voice of winter itself, the season made flesh and straw, demanding readiness.

This ecological grounding also explains why the Namahage have outlasted many of their counterparts. In regions where environmental pressures eased, rituals faded. Industrialization and modern housing reduced the risk of fire; purification practices became optional when medicine advanced. But snow in Akita still falls as heavily as ever, and depopulation has made vigilance no less urgent. The figure of the Namahage retains its relevance because the landscape continues to demand discipline. Even when the ritual is performed now partly for tourists, the ecological backdrop makes its symbolism resonate. Outsiders may see only spectacle; locals recognize the voice of their climate in the horns at the door.

From a broader perspective, this pattern illustrates a general truth: fear rituals survive where they remain ecologically legible. A society invents forms that dramatize its most pressing dangers. The ritual shocks participants into awareness of those dangers and reinforces the habits needed to counter them. Where the environment no longer threatens in the same way, the ritual can persist only as memory or entertainment. But where the danger endures, the ritual retains force. The Namahage are exemplary in this regard. They are not relics of a vanished world but dramatizations of a danger that still shapes life in Akita.

To see fear in this ecological light is to understand it as a mode of environmental pedagogy. Children may not grasp abstract discussions of fire safety, food scarcity, or impurity. But they understand the terror of a horned visitor who demands diligence. The ritual translates ecology into psychology, environment into pedagogy. Fear is the bridge between landscape and behavior, ensuring that the lessons of survival do not remain theoretical but are embodied, unforgettable, and binding.

Section 6: The Paradox of Safety through Terror

Perhaps the most striking feature of the Namahage ritual is its paradoxical structure. The figures who terrify children are, beneath the mask, their protectors. Fathers, uncles, or neighbors don straw cloaks and horns, yet they do so not to harm but to ensure safety. Terror is staged in order to preserve comfort. In this inversion lies the peculiar genius of ritual fear: it frightens not out of malice but out of care. The same hands that grasp a child's shoulders in accusation will, minutes later, hold the child close in reassurance. The paradox is deliberate, and it is precisely what allows the ritual to endure.

The ethical tension is evident. Is it right to terrify children for the sake of discipline? By modern standards of parenting, such practices can appear questionable, even abusive. Yet within the context of Oga's villages, the fear is proportioned. It is bounded in time, structured by tradition, and followed by reconciliation. The Namahage's menace is never allowed to drift into uncontrolled cruelty. The mask comes off, the visitor departs, and the ordinary bonds of kinship reassert themselves. In this closure lies the justification: the terror is temporary, the lesson lasting, and the love behind it never in doubt.

Children themselves testify to this paradox when recalling their experiences. Many describe their initial terror in vivid detail, the horns, the booming voice, the accusation of laziness. But almost as often, they recall the comfort that followed. Parents laughed, neighbors reassured, siblings compared tears. The memory is double: terror in the moment, security in the aftermath. What remains in adulthood is not trauma but a sense of having passed through a trial, a memory of being tested and found worthy of care. Fear, in this framework, becomes a strange gift.

The paradox extends beyond the family to the community as a whole. The Namahage embody menace, but their menace is understood by all to serve collective ends. They do not single out children for cruelty; they remind everyone, parents included, of obligations. In this sense, their terror is protective of the group itself. By dramatizing danger, they secure vigilance; by enacting chaos, they restore order. The paradox is that disorder is employed to guard against greater disorder, that fright itself becomes a stabilizing force.

Such paradoxes are not unique to Oga. Many cultures have discovered that the surest way to secure safety is to stage its opposite. Initiation rites place youths in simulated peril to prepare them for real dangers. Religious ceremonies evoke images of death to affirm life. Even modern entertainments, roller coasters, horror films trade on the paradoxical pleasure of controlled fright. In Japan, the kappa, water-dwelling creatures said to drag children into rivers, offered a similar lesson. Parents frightened their children with tales of these monsters not out of cruelty, but to keep them away from treacherous currents and irrigation canals. The figure was terrifying, but its terror was protective. Like the Namahage, the kappa embodied the principle that fear can guard against real harm.

This paradox also explains why ritual fear is remembered with affection rather than bitterness. The terror is undeniable, but so is the recognition that it was delivered by those who loved and protected. The doubling of roles, parent as demon, demon as parent, imprints itself deeply. It conveys to the child, even if only unconsciously, that discipline is not separate from care but another mode of its expression. Fear is revealed as something that can emerge not only from hostility but also from responsibility.

In this light, the ethical question takes a different shape. The issue is not whether fear is inflicted but how. When bounded, purposeful, and reconciled, fear can nurture rather than harm. It can instill lessons, strengthen bonds, and prepare for danger without leaving scars. The Namahage show that terror, when carefully staged, can be a form of love, love sharpened into discipline, affection expressed through ordeal. The paradox of safety through terror is not a flaw but the very logic of the ritual.

Section 7: Closing Reflections

By tracing fear through biology, ritual form, moral pedagogy, psychology, ecology, and paradox, one theme emerges with clarity: the Namahage endure because they make fear usable. They do not merely terrify. They channel terror into lessons, bind it to memory, tailor it to environment, and reconcile it within the safety of kinship. Fear, stripped of chaos and shaped by form, becomes a resource for survival.

The Namahage demonstrate that communities need fear not in spite of its discomfort but because of it. Comfort alone cannot secure discipline; affection alone cannot ensure vigilance. A society that never stages confrontation with danger leaves its members unprepared for the dangers that inevitably arrive. By frightening children in controlled fashion, Oga ensures that they learn both the reality of threat and the reality of protection. The mask in the doorway declares that safety is not natural but made, made by effort, by responsibility, by collective vigilance.

This transformation of fear into instruction is not unique to Japan. Across the world, cultures have devised rituals that frighten in order to educate. What distinguishes the Namahage is their survival into the present, their ability to remain convincing even in an era of central heating, supermarkets, and shrinking villages. Their persistence testifies to the continuing human need for rituals that make danger visible, that turn anxiety into memory, and that reaffirm community through ordeal.

With this, the book turns to its final chapter. Having followed fear from biology to ritual, from pedagogy to paradox, what remains is to consider endurance itself: how the Namahage persist in a changing world, how their image multiplies even as their setting shifts, and what it means that the mask still waits at the threshold. Fear has been justified; now the question is why the figure of fear endures, and why we continue to need it at all.

CHAPTER 9: The Communal Frame: Order and Obligation

Section 1: The Family Under Scrutiny

The Namahage enter and summon the children to account, but the questions are never directed at them alone. Each shout strikes the household as a whole. The child may tremble, but the father and mother must respond. They bow, they negotiate, they defend. In doing so, the family is bound together under judgment. The ritual makes clear that laziness or disobedience is not only the failing of a child; it reflects on the parents and on the way the household is governed.

This is one of the strongest elements of the visit. Fear alone could leave a child isolated, but the Namahage do not simply terrify and depart. They force a response from the adults. Parents cannot remain silent while horns and straw loom over their children. They must speak on their behalf, argue that the boy has been diligent or that the girl is improving. They must show that they are attentive to the progress of their children, and that they can make promises for the year ahead. In this sense, the Namahage serve as auditors of parenting. A household that cannot defend itself reveals a weakness more frightening than any mask.

Ethnographic accounts from Oga describe this moment clearly. Parents explain to the Namahage how their children have behaved, sometimes mentioning school performance, chores, or acts of kindness. The defense is not improvised from nothing; parents prepare these words in advance. They know that the demons will demand proof of diligence, so they collect evidence: an example of rising early, of helping with firewood, of studying. The father or mother speaks, and the child hears their achievements listed in public. This recognition is important. Even under fear, the child sees that their parents notice effort and remember it. The defense is frightening, but it is also a form of praise.

Yet the ritual also contains rebuke. Parents may admit shortcomings. They may tell the Namahage that their son is stubborn or that their daughter has been careless. They admit these things not only to appease the demons but also to signal to the wider community, represented by the masks, that they will correct them. It is a way of taking responsibility without losing face. The Namahage become a safe outlet for confession. A father can say his son has been lazy without shaming him directly; the blame is shifted onto the exchange with the demons. The ritual gives voice to truths that might otherwise fester in silence.

Children often remember the fear of horns and shouting most vividly, but in interviews many adults recall the way their parents defended them. Some describe feeling pride even in the midst of terror. The Namahage's roar was unbearable, but behind it was the steady voice of a parent insisting that the child was good, or at least capable of becoming better. The child learns that they are not abandoned. Fear isolates, but the parent's voice restores connection.

This pattern repeats across every household. It is not enough for one family to discipline their children quietly. The ritual makes the discipline public, binding it to the rhythm of the community. The Namahage's questions are accusatory, but they also set a stage for parental reassurance. A mother's promise that her child will study harder is not simply words to a mask; it is a vow to neighbors, ancestors, and the year ahead. The family unit becomes visible in its responsibility.

The symbolism is clear. The Namahage stand at the threshold between wilderness and home, between chaos and order.

The parents stand between the Namahage and the children. This alignment creates layers of protection and accountability. The child sees that their parent is the buffer. The parent sees that the community, embodied in the demons, expects vigilance. And the community sees that the ritual continues to hold families to account. Each layer reinforces the others.

Some observers have noted how different this is from private discipline in many modern societies. In Oga, the Namahage visit is not simply about teaching children to obey. It is about holding parents to their duty, ensuring that responsibility does not drift. The shouting and pounding are theatrical, but beneath them lies a serious demand: raise your children well, keep your household in order, contribute to the community. A family that fails to do this risks not only shame but the erosion of trust that allows a village to endure harsh winters together.

Even today, families in Oga describe the sense of reassurance that comes after the demons leave. The fear is real, but so is the relief. Parents feel they have renewed their vows in front of their children and neighbors. Children feel both the sting of fear and the comfort of protection. And the community, having heard the same pounding at every door, feels the solidarity of shared scrutiny.

The Namahage, then, are not only figures of menace. They are catalysts that force parents and children into a moment of honesty. They demand that families say aloud what they might prefer to leave unspoken: that a child has been lazy, or diligent, or defiant, or kind. By demanding words, the ritual transforms private behavior into public accountability. And by leaving after those words are spoken, the Namahage ensure that the family must live with the promises made in their presence.

In this way, the visit is both frightening and affirming. It unsettles the household, but it also reinforces bonds within it.

The child sees fear made flesh, but also loyalty made audible. The parent bows to the mask, but also claims the child as their own. This balance is why the Namahage endure. They terrify, but they also reassure. They accuse, but they also allow families to defend. In that defense lies the strength of the household, and by extension, the strength of the community.

Section 2: Shame and Accountability

The Namahage ritual is not only a matter of family discipline. It is equally a mechanism of community discipline, rooted in the Japanese cultural framework of shame. In the villages of the Oga Peninsula, where every household once participated, the Namahage were not selective visitors. They traditionally entered every home, from the poorest fisherman's hut to the mayor's house. Participation was expected; avoiding the pounding at the door would have been exceptional. This near-universality was deliberate. It prevented any family from being marked as uniquely flawed. By enduring the same accusations, every household shared the same burden of shame.

The nature of shame in Japan has long been noted by observers. It is not solely an individual experience, but a social one. The Japanese word *haji* refers to shame, disgrace or embarrassment, but it implies exposure before others rather than private guilt. The concept of *seken*, often translated as "the social gaze," captures this sense even more precisely. People live not only for themselves but in constant awareness of how they are perceived by neighbors, relatives, and community. The Namahage embody *seken*. When they accuse a child of laziness, it is not only the child who feels the weight of those words. It is the entire household, because laziness reflects on the parents, the grandparents, and by extension, the reputation of the family within the village.

The structure of the ritual ensures that shame is distributed evenly. Every door is knocked upon, every child questioned, every parent made to defend. The mayor's son is asked the same questions as the fisherman's daughter. This equal treatment reinforces the idea that discipline is not a private matter but a collective one. If only some families were visited, the ritual would create division and stigma. By visiting all, the ritual prevents isolation and instead produces solidarity. Shame becomes bearable when it is shared.

The accusations themselves are always phrased as questions. The Namahage do not declare that a child is lazy or disobedient. They ask: "Are there lazy children here? Are there children who disobey?" These questions place the burden on the family to answer. Silence is dangerous, and denial is risky, so the parents must respond. In their answers, they not only protect their children but also signal to the community that they are attentive and committed to improvement. A parent who refuses to answer would be seen as neglectful, and that neglect would spread shame far beyond the household walls.

Anthropologists studying Oga have described the Namahage as ritual auditors. They arrive once a year to examine the moral accounts of each household. The pounding and shouting may look chaotic, but the underlying structure is precise. They ask the same questions at every house, ensuring that discipline is measured across the whole community. Each household gives its report in the form of promises and confessions. The ritual is a performance, but it is also an inspection. It reaffirms the community's standards by making them visible, loud, and embodied.

The effect of this ritual audit is powerful. In interviews, residents of Oga have described the relief that follows the visit. The terror is real, but when the door closes behind the demons, the household feels purified. Parents know that they have met their obligation to the community by answering, and children know that they are held to a standard larger than their family. The village knows that every house has endured the same ordeal. This shared experience prevents the erosion of standards. If one family were lenient while others remained strict, discipline would fracture. The Namahage prevent that division by making accountability universal.

It is also important to note that shame here is not simply punitive. It is corrective. The accusations are loud and frightening, but they are followed by negotiation and promises. The purpose is not to humiliate permanently but to force acknowledgment and change. In this sense, the Namahage embody a constructive form of shame, one that restores rather than destroys. A family may feel embarrassed as the demons shout about laziness, but they leave the encounter with renewed determination to do better. The shame lingers, but it lingers as motivation.

Within the broader cultural context, the Namahage can be seen as an exaggerated version of everyday Japanese discipline. Silence, indirectness, and avoidance of confrontation often mark social interaction in Japan. Neighbors may notice idleness or disobedience but choose not to comment directly. The Namahage give voice to what is normally unspoken. They shout what others only think. In doing so, they keep the balance between social harmony and discipline. By placing the confrontation into a ritual, the community can express disapproval without risking personal conflict. The mask allows harsh words to be spoken without lasting resentment.

The fear experienced by children is genuine, but the pressure on parents is equally significant. They are reminded that their role is not only private but public. To raise children poorly is to risk the standing of the entire household. The Namahage dramatize this truth in a way that cannot be ignored. The pounding on the door is more than noise; it is the sound of the community checking whether the family has upheld its end of the social contract.

In this light, the Namahage ritual can be understood as a form of social glue. It binds families together not just internally but horizontally, across the village. Every household is held to the same standard, and every household participates in the same fear and relief. The shared shame ensures that discipline is not optional but collective. It is a way of saying that survival in a harsh landscape requires not only effort but cooperation, and that cooperation is impossible without accountability.

Section 3: The Social Contract of Fear

When the Namahage pound on the door, they are not only frightening children. They are renewing the invisible agreement that holds the village together. This agreement is not written, but its terms are widely understood. Parents are expected to raise their children with diligence. Children are expected to obey, study, and contribute to the household. Each family is expected to work, to keep order, and to support neighbors. In return, the community shares the burdens of survival: watching over one another's children, lending labor in the fields, helping rebuild after storms. The Namahage dramatize this exchange. Their presence is a reminder that the contract must be honored, and that neglect threatens not only one family but all.

The ritual is staged as confrontation, but its deeper function is reassurance. When the demons visit every house, pounding and shouting, the entire community sees that standards have been applied equally. A father knows that his neighbor also faced the same accusations, and that his children too were called to account. This shared ordeal reinforces fairness. It prevents suspicion that one family is being lenient while others are strict, or that one household has slipped into idleness while others labor. The Namahage make visible the discipline that every family is supposed to maintain in private. By doing so, they remove the danger of envy or resentment.

This dynamic is particularly important in small villages where survival depends on cooperation. Winter closes roads, buries fields, and makes outside support unreliable. A family that grows complacent does not only risk itself; it becomes a liability to its neighbors. If one household neglects its duties, the community must compensate. The Namahage prevent this by insisting that no family can hide behind closed doors. The pounding announces that accountability is public. The shouting makes clear that idleness is not just a personal failure but a threat to the group.

The fear is therefore not random but structured. It is contained within the ritual's boundaries, yet it presses deeply enough to remind everyone of their obligations. Children cry, but they also learn that their parents stand between them and the demons. Parents bow, but they also learn that their neighbors expect vigilance. Each action is symbolic of a larger truth: order must be maintained if the community is to endure.

Some anthropologists have called this ritual a form of social contract enacted through theater. The questions shouted by the Namahage are accusations, but they are also the terms of the contract spoken aloud. Are there lazy children here? Do you obey your parents? These are not merely inquiries about one household; they are the foundation of the village's stability. By answering, parents reaffirm their agreement to raise responsible children, to contribute labor, and to uphold standards. By bowing and thanking the demons, they show that they accept the authority of the community to inspect their private life.

Fear functions here as a kind of binding agent. It turns abstract obligations into felt experience. Promises made in calm conversation might be forgotten, but promises made under the eyes of a mask and the roar of a voice carry weight. The heart pounds, the child trembles, the parent defends. These physical sensations anchor the words. The memory of fear ensures that the agreement lingers long after the straw has been swept away.

Even the sequence of the ritual reflects the logic of the contract. Accusation comes first, establishing the problem. Negotiation follows, where parents and demons discuss the child's conduct. Instruction comes next, where clear commands are issued. Finally comes release, where promises are accepted and the demons depart. Each stage mirrors the structure of obligation: recognition of fault, acknowledgment of duty, agreement to improve, confirmation of order. What might appear chaotic to outsiders is in fact a carefully staged renewal of the community's moral contract.

The importance of this renewal cannot be overstated. In modern contexts, laws and institutions enforce discipline. But in small rural communities, especially in earlier centuries, the social contract depended on shared values, mutual surveillance, and the memory of tradition. The Namahage embodied those forces. Their pounding on the door reminded villagers that the community had eyes and ears, that no one was free to shirk responsibility. At the same time, their eventual departure reassured families that once the ritual was observed, the year could begin anew with a clean slate.

The children who experienced the fear of the Namahage often grew into the young men who donned the masks themselves. In doing so, they moved from being the subjects of discipline to the agents of it. This transition reinforced the social contract across generations. The terror they once felt became the authority they now wielded, and in enacting it, they ensured that the next generation of children would learn the same lessons. The cycle created continuity, binding the past, present, and future into a single line of accountability.

The social contract embodied in the Namahage ritual is not fragile. It is enforced with pounding fists, roaring voices, and the physical presence of straw and wood. Yet it is also subtle. It relies on shared understanding, on unspoken recognition of mutual dependence. The contract is never signed, never written, but it is renewed each year with noise, fear, and relief. By dramatizing the terms, the Namahage ensure that no one forgets them.

Section 4: Continuity Across Generations

The Namahage ritual survives not only because it frightens children, but because it binds generations together. Each person in the village participates at some stage of life, and by passing through these roles, individuals are woven into the continuity of the community.

For children, the ritual is an early encounter with fear, discipline, and belonging. They sit in the center of the room, trembling as the demons roar, while parents defend them and promise improvement. This memory imprints itself deeply. Many adults in Oga can recall in vivid detail their first encounter with the Namahage decades earlier. They remember the pounding on the door, the smell of straw, the voice booming their names. The memory is not simply fear; it is an initiation into the life of the community.

As they grow older, these same children watch the ritual from a different position. Teenagers and young adults often accompany the Namahage as helpers, carrying straw, preparing masks, or assisting with the route from house to house. At this stage, they move from passive recipients of fear to active participants in sustaining the tradition. They still remember their own terror, but now they help prepare it for others. This transition builds empathy as well as authority. They know how the children feel because they once felt the same.

When young men reach adulthood, especially before marriage, they take on the central role of becoming Namahage themselves. To wear the mask is not simply play. It is a responsibility. They must project authority, embody discipline, and carry the weight of the community's expectations. The transformation is profound. Behind the mask, a man who is usually known as a neighbor's son or a friend's cousin becomes a figure of dread. The anonymity of the costume allows him to speak with a voice that is not his own. In this way, personal identity dissolves into collective duty.

Older adults watch from yet another perspective. They may stand outside to guide the route, pour sake for the demons, or act as witnesses to the promises made. Their role is to ensure that the ritual is carried out properly, neither too harsh nor too lenient. They monitor the balance between fear and order, between chaos and discipline. By overseeing, they guard the integrity of the tradition.

The cycle is complete when those who once wore the mask become parents themselves. Now they sit in the same place where their parents once sat, defending their children against accusations. They understand both sides: the fear of the child, the responsibility of the demon, and the duty of the parent. This layered experience reinforces the continuity of the ritual. No generation is left outside it. Every person carries memories of being confronted, participating, and then defending.

The communal aspect of this cycle cannot be overstated. In small villages, people grow up together, marry within the region, and remain neighbors for life. The man behind the mask today may have been the crying child twenty years ago and will be the father bowing tomorrow. The community recognizes these transitions and values them as signs of maturity. To endure the Namahage as a child proves resilience. To wear the mask as a youth proves responsibility. To defend children as a parent proves commitment. Each role confirms belonging to the group.

This continuity is further reinforced by the seasonal rhythm of the ritual. Because the Namahage always come at the end of the year, the memory is anchored to the calendar. Children measure their growth by how they responded this year compared to last. Parents compare their household's discipline across winters. Elders remember decades of visits, the faces of past masks, and the voices of men who are no longer alive. The ritual therefore serves as a timekeeper for the community. It counts not only years but lives.

Continuity also protects the ritual against outside change. Modernization, migration, and the spread of tourism have influenced Oga, but the core of the Namahage remains intact because the cycle of roles renews itself. Even as young people leave for cities, those who remain inherit the responsibility of wearing the mask. In this way, the ritual endures because it is built into the fabric of community life. It is not dependent on a single generation but carried by the ongoing participation of all.

The Namahage thus provide more than a night of fear. They provide a framework for belonging across time. A child's tears, a youth's hidden grin behind a mask, a parent's bowed head, and an elder's watchful gaze are all part of the same pattern. This cycle is what gives the ritual its strength. It is not a performance staged for others but a tradition that each person must live, again and again, from one role to the next.

The continuity across generations ensures that the ritual never becomes distant folklore. It remains lived experience, binding the present to the past and preparing the future. Each role carries lessons that cannot be taught by words alone. Fear teaches children humility. Wearing the mask teaches young adults responsibility. Defending children teaches parents accountability. Watching over the ritual teaches elders stewardship. Together, these roles maintain the coherence of the community.

Section 5: Reflection: Fear as Social Glue

The Namahage ritual reveals how fear can be transformed from a destabilizing force into a stabilizing one. In most contexts, fear isolates. It drives people apart, pits them against one another, or leaves them paralyzed. In Oga, fear does the opposite. It draws households closer together, reinforces parental roles, and binds neighbors into a shared rhythm. The pounding on the door is frightening, but it is also a reminder that no family is alone in its discipline or its struggles.

This transformation rests on two conditions: structure and universality. Structure means that the fear is contained within a ritual. The demons arrive on a set night, perform their accusations, and depart. There is no uncertainty about whether the ritual will happen, only about how intense the visit will be. The fear is sharp but limited, framed by tradition. Universality means that every household endures the same ordeal. There is no singling out, no stigma, no family left untouched. The fear is spread evenly, so that it becomes collective rather than isolating.

When fear is both structured and universal, it ceases to be destructive and becomes a kind of glue. It presses families together inside their homes as parents shield children and promise to the demons. It presses households together across the village as neighbors know that the same pounding and shouting echoes in every lane. The ritual binds people not in spite of fear but through it.

For children, this binding is felt most immediately. They cling to their parents during the visit, finding protection in the arms that shield them. The terror of the mask is matched by the reassurance of the parent's defense. The experience etches into memory not only the fear of the demon but the presence of the family that stood against it. In later years, adults often recall not just the horned face that frightened them but the sight of their father bowing or their mother promising improvement. Fear and care are woven together, creating a bond that outlasts both.

For parents, the ritual is equally binding. They are forced to confront their responsibilities in front of their children and in front of the community. The accusations from the Namahage leave no space for evasion. Parents must answer, defend, and commit. In this way, the ritual deepens their role. They are not only protectors of their children but representatives of their household before the community. Their children witness this defense and learn that parental authority is both duty and sacrifice. The parent's words in that moment carry a weight that ordinary scolding does not.

For the community as a whole, the shared fear ensures continuity. Every family feels the same pounding, hears the same questions, and makes the same promises. This common ordeal levels differences of status and wealth. For one night, the fisherman's hut and the mayor's house are equal before the demons. The ritual reminds everyone that survival is not a matter of individual success but of collective vigilance. Fear serves as the lever that equalizes, uniting the community through common vulnerability.

The Namahage also highlight the paradox of fear as a moral tool. Fear alone can corrode, but fear framed within ritual teaches discipline and responsibility. The difference lies in control. The pounding is terrifying, but everyone knows it will end. The shouting is harsh, but everyone knows it will not last forever. This containment allows the lesson to remain while the terror fades. What lingers is not despair but resolve.

Anthropologists often describe rituals as mechanisms for channeling chaos into order. The Namahage are a vivid example. They embody chaos, the roar, the pounding, the wild masks, but their actions restore order. They accuse, extract promises, and depart, leaving the household more disciplined than before. The chaos is staged precisely so that order can be renewed. Without the roar, the silence afterward would not feel as binding.

Fear as social glue is not unique to Oga, but the Namahage illustrate it with clarity. The ritual shows that fear can be communal rather than divisive, constructive rather than destructive. It demonstrates that in a small, vulnerable community, survival depends not only on labor and resources but on shared standards, renewed publicly and dramatically. The demons' fists on the door are frightening, but they are also the sound of the community reminding itself that it must hold together.

The endurance of the Namahage across centuries suggests that this use of fear has worked. Generations have grown up trembling under the gaze of the masks and then grown strong enough to wear them. Families have endured the accusations and then found reassurance in making promises. Villages have gathered around the ritual and carried it forward despite social and economic change. The glue has held.

In the end, the Namahage are less about demons and more about the ties between people. The straw, the masks, the shouting, all are tools to shape behavior and memory. What remains after the visit is not only the echo of fear but the sense of belonging it enforces. The ritual teaches that no one is exempt, that all are bound by the same rules, and that only by accepting those rules together can the community survive another winter.

CHAPTER 10: Other Demons at the Door

Section 1: Introduction

Across Japan, in regions far removed from Akita, figures resembling the Namahage appear in their own seasonal rituals. These beings do not all share the same masks, words, or exact customs, but they occupy a similar place in the rhythm of the year: they arrive at the threshold of the household, they confront the family, and they embody the authority of the community. Some are thought of as demons, others as gods, and in a few traditions they carry both aspects at once. What unites them is the act of visitation itself. Each year, often at the turn of the year or at another charged moment in the seasonal calendar, the ordinary door of a home opens to admit something that does not belong to everyday life.

It is important to note that these rituals are not mere variations of the Namahage. They developed in different regions, each shaped by its own geography, economy, and religious history. While the Namahage of Oga are wrapped in straw and famous for their terrifying masks, the Toshidon of Kagoshima wear different costumes and balance severity with blessings. The Amamehagi of Ishikawa confront laziness with gestures unique to their community, even as they echo some of the same moral themes. To treat these as copies of one another would flatten their richness. Each tradition deserves attention in its own right.

At the same time, their coexistence across distant prefectures suggests a broader Japanese pattern. In an archipelago marked by mountains, storms, and isolation, rural communities devised rituals that reminded households of discipline and renewal. Though the details vary, many of these customs take place at the end of the year, when families are gathered indoors, when provisions must be rationed, and when the coming season demands resolve. The figures at the door are not random inventions. They are responses to shared conditions of survival and the shared human need to embody morality in visible, dramatic form.

This chapter turns to those other visitors: the Toshidon of Kagoshima in the far south, the Amamehagi of Ishikawa on the Noto Peninsula, and smaller local practices scattered across the country. Each will be described in its own context, with its own meanings, before any comparisons are drawn. By looking outward from Oga, the Namahage can be seen not as an isolated oddity, but as part of a wider cultural landscape where demons and gods remind people of their duties.

Section 2: Toshidon of Kagoshima

Far to the south of Oga, on the remote Koshikijima Islands of Kagoshima Prefecture, there is another ritual in which demons walk through the night. Here they are called Toshidon, and like the Namahage, they appear at the threshold of homes on New Year's Eve, demanding to know whether children have been obedient. The geography could not be more different. Where Oga is defined by snow and the hard edge of the Sea of Japan, Koshikijima lies in the warmer waters of southern Kyushu, its coastline softer, its winters mild enough that fields still hold greenery when the year turns. Yet the ritual impulse is the same: to personify authority, to summon fear, and to guide children through a passage of accountability as one year ends and another begins.

The Toshidon figures are distinct in appearance. Rather than the towering, horned faces of Oga, Toshidon wear straw capes over layered garments and carved wooden masks painted in vivid colors. Their faces glare with fierce eyes and wide mouths, generally less fang-like than Oga's, and they often carry wooden staves or bundles. The atmosphere, too, differs. Where Namahage can thunder into a home as if storm and sea had taken human form, Toshidon are received with a blend of awe and expectation. Children kneel before them, and what follows is not only accusation but blessing.

The ritual centers on dialogue. Each child is called forward and questioned about behavior in the past year. Were they diligent in their studies? Did they listen to their parents? Did they help with chores? The tone is stern, but it is coupled with reassurance. After the questioning comes the reward: each child receives mochi, a token not only of approval but of good fortune for the year to come. In this gesture the ritual reveals its double edge. Fear is present, but it is immediately softened by generosity. The Toshidon embody both warning and care, figures who correct but also encourage.

Adults who grew up with the ritual often describe it as one of their clearest childhood memories. The sound of the door sliding open, the sudden appearance of the masked figure, the moment of being called by name, these are recollections that remain vivid decades later. Some speak of trembling with fear, clutching their mother's sleeve, heart racing. Others remember the pride of receiving mochi after enduring the questioning, a sense that they had passed a test. In these memories, the fear never quite fades, but it is tempered by gratitude. The ritual was not only about punishment but about recognition.

The gift of mochi itself carries weight. Mochi is central to Japanese New Year customs, symbolizing renewal, resilience, and continuity. It is a food that binds the old year to the new, made by pounding rice into a substance both pliable and enduring. To receive it from the hands of a Toshidon is to receive more than a sweet, it is to be handed the promise of growth and perseverance. In this sense, the ritual teaches that discipline and reward are inseparable. Children must answer for their actions, but they are also acknowledged as part of the community's future.

Unlike the Namahage, who visit every house in Oga, the Toshidon tradition is confined to the islands of Koshikijima, giving it a strong sense of place. The entire community participates, and preparation begins well before the night itself. Children are warned, just as in Oga, that the figures will know their faults. Parents prepare offerings and ensure that the ritual unfolds smoothly. Young men, chosen to wear the costumes, undergo instruction to ensure that the questions and blessings are delivered properly. The ritual is thus highly structured, balancing severity with ceremony.

The contrast with Namahage is striking but instructive. Namahage are figures of disruption, bursting into homes with pounding fists and booming voices. Toshidon, though stern, carry with them a sense of order and continuity. Where Namahage emphasize shame, Toshidon emphasize correction followed by encouragement. Both frighten, but the fright serves different proportions of discipline and reassurance. In this way, the rituals reveal regional variations in how communities approached the same fundamental concern: how to shape children into responsible members of society through the drama of ritualized fear.

For the children, what mattered was not the theological origin of the figures or the academic interpretation of their symbolism, but the immediacy of the experience. To hear their name called by a voice not quite human, to feel the weight of being watched and judged, and then to hold the warm mochi in their hands, these were moments that made the abstract expectations of parents and teachers suddenly tangible. Adults who recall

Toshidon often describe the ritual not as cruel but as formative. The fear was real, but it was bounded, softened by community, and resolved in blessing.

The persistence of Toshidon on Koshikijima, despite modernization and population decline, speaks to the depth of its meaning. It is not a relic performed for outsiders, but a living practice still recognized by those who grew up with it as essential to the rhythm of the year. The figures remain stern, the children still tremble, and the mochi continues to pass from masked hand to small hand as a bridge between past and future.

Section 3: Amamehagi of Ishikawa

The Amamehagi tradition of Ishikawa Prefecture, centered in the Noto Peninsula, shares a kinship with the Namahage of Akita, but it is distinguished by its own history, timing, and symbolism. The name itself reveals its function. The term *amame* refers to the calluses or sores that appear on the skin of those who sit idly by the hearth for too long, much like the *namomi* of Akita. The word *hagi* means "to peel away." Together, *amamehagi* signals the role of the masked figures: to scrape off idleness, to expose the danger of sloth, and to remind households that survival requires diligence. Like the Namahage, the figures serve as auditors of conduct, appearing in disguise to confront the community with its own moral obligations.

Unlike the Namahage, which storm through homes on New Year's Eve, the Amamehagi traditionally arrive on the fifteenth day of the first lunar month, a date linked to older agrarian calendars rather than the Gregorian system that governs Japan today. This timing, deep in winter, was not arbitrary. It came after the initial festival of the year but before preparations for spring planting began. In villages across Noto, this midwinter visit reinforced the idea that one must shake off winter idleness and ready the body and household for the coming agricultural cycle. Farmers saw the ritual as an essential act of seasonal renewal, ensuring that laziness did not harden into habit during the long nights when snow cut them off from fields and sea.

The setting of Noto shaped the character of Amamehagi. The peninsula juts into the Sea of Japan, exposed to gales and heavy snows but also sustained by fishing and terrace farming. Households were small, villages tightly bound together by necessity, and isolation was common in winter. In such conditions, a ritual of visitation carried particular weight. When the masked figures crossed thresholds, they brought not only fear but also the reassurance that each family was part of a larger order, watched and bound by the same discipline.

The costumes of the Amamehagi bore resemblance to those of the Namahage, yet their style reflected local craft. Masks were often carved from paulownia or other lightweight woods, then lacquered and painted. Their features tended toward severity: angular brows, bulging eyes, mouths stretched wide in expressions that blurred command with menace. Horns were common but not universal. Some masks emphasized the grotesque through color, deep reds, blacks, or ochres, while others were plainer, relying on exaggerated carving to instill unease. Costumes were made of straw capes, like the *mino* of Akita, which rustled and shed snow when the figures moved inside homes. The sound of straw on wood and the sudden invasion of bulk into narrow rooms were as unsettling here as in Oga.

The choreography of the visit was also familiar. The Amamehagi pounded on doors, shouted accusations, and entered homes to question children. Their first concern was idleness, framed through the metaphor of skin lesions: had anyone grown the *amame* of laziness? Were there children neglecting their studies, disobeying their parents, or refusing to help with chores? Like the Namahage, they shouted their questions, often in dialect, so that even the smallest child could not pretend ignorance. Parents defended their children, bowed, promised improvement, and offered sake. The performance was both terrifying and formulaic, known yet unpredictable, its impact residing in repetition across generations.

What distinguished the Amamehagi further was the timing of their departure. The fifteenth day of the first month was also associated with the *koshi matsuri* or "small New Year" festivals in parts of Japan, when ancestral spirits were believed to visit households. In this broader ritual context, the Amamehagi could be seen not only as demons or enforcers but as agents of purification, ensuring that families were ready to receive blessings by discarding bad habits. In some villages, the Amamehagi would even collect offerings from households, rice cakes, sake, or other tokens, echoing the give-and-take between human and spirit that defined so much of Japanese ritual practice.

Accounts from the twentieth century describe how children experienced the Amamehagi with the same mixture of dread and memory that Oga's children felt toward the Namahage. Ethnographers recorded that adults who had been visited as children could still recall the pounding on the door and the sensation of straw brushing their arms, decades later. The ritual etched itself into memory precisely because it blurred the line between theater and reality. Even though every child eventually learned who had worn the mask, the memory of the night remained visceral, as if the mask itself had carried truth beyond its disguise.

By the late twentieth century, however, the Amamehagi ritual had begun to decline. Urbanization drew younger villagers to cities, leaving fewer unmarried men to serve as the figures. The disruption of traditional calendars under the influence of modern schooling and work also eroded the timing of the event. In some places, the visits were condensed, reinterpreted, or abandoned altogether. Festivals staged for tourists sometimes replaced intimate household visits, echoing the pattern seen in Akita with the Namahage. Yet the cultural meaning persisted. Local governments and preservation societies in Ishikawa began to document the tradition, record oral histories, and, in some towns, sponsor revived performances. Even if the ritual shifted from lived practice to staged heritage, the figure of the Amamehagi retained its symbolic force as a reminder of the region's values.

Modern observers sometimes compare the Namahage and Amamehagi as regional variations of a shared archetype: the winter demon who arrives to discipline children and reassert communal order. But the differences are as significant as the similarities. Oga's Namahage stride into homes on the most liminal night of the year, when one year turns into the next, confronting families at the threshold of time. The Amamehagi, by contrast, arrive two weeks later, aligned with the agricultural cycle rather than the calendar year. Their very presence insists on readiness for the tasks ahead, connecting moral discipline to physical labor in the fields. Both figures strip away laziness, but one does so at the hinge of the calendar, the other at the hinge of the farming season.

The strength of the Amamehagi tradition lies in its capacity to adapt while preserving its central message. Even in villages where the household visits have dwindled, the memory of the ritual persists in stories, photographs, and community identity. Local children still learn about the Amamehagi in school lessons or during cultural festivals, ensuring that the figure remains part of their imagination. The rough mask and the pounding at the door continue to symbolize the same lesson: that idleness is dangerous, that effort is necessary, and that the community has the right to call its members to account.

In this way, the Amamehagi remain a living counterpart to the Namahage, distinct in timing and performance but united in purpose. Both embody the winter demon as a moral instructor, a figure who intrudes not to destroy but to demand renewal. The straw cape, the carved mask, the booming voice, these are not relics of a distant past but echoes of a truth that still resonates. Survival requires vigilance. Communities endure only when effort is shared. And the reminder, however frightening, must come from outside the family, carried on the shoulders of masked figures who embody the authority of tradition.

Section 4: Paantu of Miyako Island

If the northern coast of Honshu produced horned demons wrapped in straw, the southern islands of Okinawa gave rise to a very different intruder. On Miyako Island, far to the south of Kyushu, villagers still stage the Paantu, one of Japan's most tactile ritual survivals. It does not arrive at New Year but in the ninth month of the lunar calendar, when visiting deities appear caked in mud and leaves to bless, frighten, and protect.

On Miyako the best-known rite is Paantu Punaha in the Shimajiri district. Three men from the community are chosen. They bind vines around their bodies, fasten roughly carved wooden masks to their faces, and coat themselves in thick black mud drawn from a sacred spring known locally as Nmariga. The figures move slowly and heavily, carrying branches that serve both as prop and applicator. They smear mud on doors, walls, cars, clothes, and skin, leaving streaks and handprints that certify a household has been visited.

The masks themselves are coarse and effective. Most show a high brow, narrow eyes, and a thin or leering mouth cut into the wood. Under the glare, the mud reads not as mess but as power. The texture clings to hair and cloth. It cracks as it dries, leaving a map of the route on every touched surface. New houses and newborns are sought out first, since an early anointing is considered a good beginning.

The Paantu do not ask permission. They enter lanes, courtyards, and thresholds, and everyone becomes fair game. Children flee shrieking until their cheeks and sleeves are streaked with clay. Adults wipe at their faces but laugh while doing so. The shock is real, the welcome is real, and the contradiction is the point. A blessing that behaves like a pursuit makes its meaning hard to forget. Handprints dry on door panels and stay for days as proof that the household has been reached by something outside the ordinary.

Within Japan, Paantu is part of a wider family of "visiting deity" rites called raiho-shin, in which masked figures go house to house admonishing laziness, warning children, and renewing the year. In 2018 that complex of practices, including Paantu on Miyako, was inscribed by UNESCO on the Representative List of the Intangible Cultural Heritage of Humanity. The listing recognized what villagers already knew: that these visits are not theater but a seasonal obligation, and that the community's discipline is strengthened by a face that arrives from outside daily life.

Paantu is not unique even within Miyako. Some neighborhoods involve noro priestesses or local shrine personnel in the preparations, while others keep the rite squarely in the hands of designated male performers. What remains constant is the contact. Where Namahage tests a family with questions and glare, Paantu confirms a blessing by touch. The mud is the message.

The route is practical as well as symbolic. The figures move through new subdivisions to mark fresh construction, then back into older lanes where doors stand open and families wait for the knock that is not a knock. The air smells of wet earth and crushed vine. You hear it before you see it: branches scraping plaster, rubber sandals on concrete, a burst of laughter that turns to a squeal. In narrow entryways the Paantu fills the space. The mask crowds the field of view and the mud finishes the conversion from visitor to deity.

Like all living rituals, Paantu has had to negotiate the present. As more outsiders arrive to watch or photograph, communities have set expectations so that participation does not turn into confrontation. The rite remains what it has always been for locals: a necessary mess that purifies a place for another year. The figures come caked in the island's own earth and leave it on every surface they touch. Terror and protection arrive together and cannot be separated.

Section 5: Kasedori of Yamagata

Far to the north, in snowbound Yamagata Prefecture, another visitor takes shape as the Kasedori. Young men wrap themselves in heavy cloaks of rice straw that hang like thick feathers, then pull on pointed hoods that suggest beaks. Ropes cinch the bundles tight. The layers muffle their voices into a rasping cry as they move through the streets, and the straw rustles with every step.

The Kasedori appear in early February, when the agricultural year is starting to stir beneath the snow. In Kaminoyama the day begins at the castle grounds, where the costumed figures gather before setting off through the town. They call out as they go, a harsh bird call, and the sound carries down alleys before the procession arrives. Spectators line the route with buckets and ladles. As the Kasedori pass, people splash them with water, a gesture believed to guard the hearth, the storehouse, and the family for the year ahead. In the cold air the straw darkens and drips, and for a moment steam hangs above the masked faces.

The charge is practical: in wooden towns one stray spark can erase a street. The soaking is an enacted wish that the year will pass without flame. It is also an offering of prosperity. Traders and innkeepers step outside to throw water at the straw birds and shout for good business. Households wait with doors open and a towel ready for a child who has edged too close to be missed by the splash.

Preparation begins weeks ahead in barns that smell of dried rice straw and rope. Straw is bundled and woven into thick panels that hang in layered fringe. Elders show younger men how to lash the panels to the torso and hips, how to twist rope strong enough to hold when soaked, and how to shape the pointed hood so the beak keeps its line in the wind. The costume is heavy and deliberately awkward. It slows the pace and turns a person into a moving bundle that reads as a bird from a distance. During the route, handlers walk alongside with spare rope and a knife to retie loosened lashings. When the day ends, the suits are dried, repaired, and stored, and the knowledge passes to the next group who will learn the call, the pace, and the responsibility that comes with being splashed for the town's safety.

Children crowd the edges, half thrilled and half wary. They tug small strands from the straw and pocket them for luck. In older accounts those pieces were tied into brooms or tucked near cooking fires as a quiet shield against embers. The costume sheds as it travels, and those small leavings carry the visit into kitchens and workshops long after the procession has passed.

The bird form is not a whim. It couples fire prevention to fertility, linking the safety of the hearth to the health of the fields. Water meets straw, winter meets the first hint of spring, and the town accepts a soaking in exchange for another year of vigilance. Here the visiting figure is not an accusing demon but a messenger of renewal. The lesson is plain: keep watch or fire will undo labor.

Kasedori works by presence rather than pursuit. The figures do not chase children through alleyways, and they do not interrogate households at the threshold. They move steadily, accept water, and keep moving. The circuit marks the town as noticed and bound into the season. Where Paantu blesses by touch and Namahage compels by glare and voice, Kasedori teaches by procession and by the shock of cold water on straw. What lingers after they pass is the sound of rustle and splash, and the sense that vigilance is a shared duty.

Section 6: Patterns and Persistence

From the mud of Miyako to the straw of Yamagata, these visitations show how communities rely on a figure from outside daily life to carry danger and renewal into the home. Place shapes method. Subtropical islands bless by touch. Snow country warns by water and straw. Peninsulas confront idleness in midwinter. The details change, the function holds steady. An ordinary door opens, and a face that is not a neighbor's steps through to set the year in order.

The pattern has echoes far from Japan. Alpine streets once hosted horned winter visitors, and British villages sent costumed guisers into gatherings. The hinge of the year works the same way in many places. There is a short, licensed intrusion that jolts the house so that order can be secured again. What makes the Japanese rites distinctive is how closely the universal shape is tied to local ground. Mud is taken from a named spring, straw is cut from nearby fields, questions are shouted in a dialect children know by ear. The form is shared, the texture is particular.

Endurance rests on more than belief. It rests on habits. These nights recur on fixed dates. People prepare without being told. Costumes are woven, repaired, and stored. Routes are remembered by turn and doorway. Roles are handed down: who wears, who handles, who opens the door first, who answers. Even the call is learned as a sound before it is learned as words. When a rite is built into this many small tasks, it becomes hard to cancel. The calendar carries it forward because hands are already moving.

Fear is present, but it is calibrated. The visitor is frightening, yet bounded by rules. He arrives at night and leaves the same night. He does not break furniture or strike, he does not stay to argue. He confronts and marks and moves on. Children are named and judged, then released. Adults are pressed to answer, then thanked. The family is shaken, not shattered. That proportion keeps the rite from turning into cruelty. It also makes memory do the teaching later, when fear has cooled but the lesson remains.

Modern life pushes on these customs from every side. Populations shrink, schools and work drift off the old calendar, and cameras turn a threshold into a stage. Communities answer in practical ways. They shorten routes but keep the night. They train younger wearers earlier in the year. They draw lines for visitors so that watching does not replace being visited. Even where a festival version has grown around the rite, households still keep a smaller practice at home. The show can help the custom survive, but the household visit is what keeps it real.

Within this landscape, the Namahage of Oga remain unusually present. Each New Year's Eve still brings the thud of boots and voices at the door. Horned masks fill narrow rooms. Straw sheds snow onto tatami. The questions come in a simple vocabulary that children learn young. Are you lazy. Do you obey. Do you work. The force lies in being named in front of family, then sent into the new year with the demand to do better.

Oga endures for reasons beyond fame. There is an economy of craft that keeps masks in circulation, committees that keep the route, and households that expect to be tested. The rite is sharp by design. Paantu blesses by touch. Kasedori reassures by water and straw. Namahage accuses, then leaves. Few tokens remain, often just a scatter of straw, but memory is the hardest thing to misplace. That edge has helped Oga hold the line between a night of ritual and a night of spectacle.

What ties these practices together is not theory but the act itself. A door slides open. The room becomes a stage. For a few minutes the family belongs to a story larger than itself. When the visitor leaves, the house is the same and not the same. Mud dries on the lintel, straw cools on the floor, a child breathes again, and the year has been marked. That is how these rites persist. They live because people keep doing them, and because being visited, once felt, is hard to forget.

CHAPTER 11: From Ritual to Performance and Icon

Section 1: Introduction

The Namahage are best known for their house-to-house visits on the night of December 31, when masked figures wrapped in straw burst into homes, roaring questions at children and scolding parents for neglect. That ritual has been at the heart of the Oga Peninsula for centuries, intimate in its setting and visceral in its impact. To face the Namahage in one's own kitchen is to encounter a force that feels as though it has crossed from another world. It is private theater, and its stage is the threshold of the home.

Yet the Namahage exist today in two parallel forms. Alongside the household visits is a second, very different appearance: the Namahage Sedo Festival, held on the second weekend of February. While the December rite unfolds in darkened rooms, with neighbors crouched by the hearth, the Sedo Festival gathers crowds before shrines and bonfires. The figures descend from the mountain not to storm a household but to perform before a mass audience. The same masks and straw cloaks appear, but their setting is one of spectacle, amplified by drums and flames. In this form, the Namahage do not question a child directly or point to an idle farmer. They walk among tourists, receive applause, and pose for cameras. The transformation is striking.

The contrast between these two modes is essential for understanding what Namahage have become in the modern era. The house visit is a ritual, tied to community and carried out in private, often without outsiders present. The Sedo Festival is a performance, formally inaugurated in 1964 when Shinzan Shrine's saitosai fire rite was combined with a public staging of the Namahage, presenting the tradition to a broader audience while supporting its continuation. In effect, one ritual faces inward, policing and protecting households, while the other faces outward, presenting the Namahage as cultural heritage. Both are authentic in different senses, but they speak to different needs.

For locals, the New Year's Eve visits remain the anchor. Children are still taught to fear the masked figures who come pounding at the door, and parents continue to use the visit as a moment of instruction. But the ritual depends on households willing to open their doors, and on younger men willing to put on the costume. As populations age and rural communities shrink, continuity becomes fragile. In this light the Sedo Festival offers a safeguard. It is public, organized, and funded, with the added legitimacy of being named a UNESCO Intangible Cultural Heritage of Humanity in 2018. Visitors from across Japan, and increasingly from abroad, come to see the festival. Its staging ensures that even if household visits fade, the Namahage will remain visible.

At the same time, the festival raises difficult questions. Does presenting the Namahage before an audience dilute their force? Can a ritual of fear survive when it is reframed as performance? For a child hiding behind a parent on New Year's Eve, the Namahage are terrifying. For a tourist standing behind a camera at Shinzan Shrine, they are curious, even entertaining. The intention has shifted from enforcement to display. What once marked the discipline of a household has become a cultural brand.

The transition is not unique to Oga. Throughout the world, rituals that once carried deep communal power have been reconfigured into spectacles for outsiders. In the Alps, Krampus now marches in parades through urban streets, drawing tourists who applaud the very figure their ancestors once dreaded. In Bulgaria, the Kukeri processions are now staged in festivals that attract international photographers. Oga's Sedo Festival belongs to this same global pattern, where fearsome visitors are recast as heritage icons. What makes the Namahage distinctive is that both forms still coexist. The intimate ritual in the home has not yet vanished. It remains alive in parallel with the staged festival, and that duality reveals much about how tradition adapts under pressure.

The existence of two Namahage traditions side by side is therefore not a contradiction but a testimony to resilience. The household visits keep the ritual embedded in lived community life. The Sedo Festival keeps the Namahage visible in the wider world and ensures institutional support for its continuation. The question is not whether one is authentic and the other false. It is whether the balance between fear and performance can be maintained without the ritual losing the essence that has allowed it to endure for centuries.

This chapter examines that balance. It will follow the festival's emergence and growth, the international recognition it has drawn, and the tensions it creates for the people of Oga. At its core lies a paradox: in order to survive, a ritual of fear must also be willing to perform.

Section 2: The Sedo Festival at Shinzan Shrine

The Sedo Festival takes place each year on the second weekend of February at Shinzan Shrine (Shinzan Jinja) in Oga City's Shinzan/Kitaura area. The event grew out of the saitosai, a fire ceremony held at mountain shrines since at least the early modern period. In 1964, local organizers decided to link this ceremony with the Namahage tradition, creating a festival that could serve both religious and cultural purposes. The result is one of

Akita's best-known winter events, drawing visitors from across Japan and beyond.

On the opening night, torches flare against the snow as drummers pound a slow, steady rhythm. Crowds gather before the shrine, wrapped in heavy coats and scarves, their breath visible in the frigid air. From the darkness at the edge of the mountain path, figures begin to emerge. They are the Namahage, wearing the same horned masks and heavy straw cloaks that villagers would recognize from their New Year's Eve visits. In the glow of firelight, the silhouettes are immense, exaggerated by the bulk of straw and the glint of painted eyes. Spectators murmur, some press forward to photograph, while children clutch their parents. The scene deliberately evokes the older village ritual but transposes it to a public stage.

The descent of the Namahage from the mountain is choreographed but retains symbolic force. In the original household visits, the Namahage arrive from the mountains as emissaries of otherworldly power. At the Sedo Festival, this moment is reproduced on a larger scale, with the figures approaching through torchlight to meet the waiting community. Their entry into the shrine grounds dramatizes the threshold between wilderness and settlement, echoing the tension that has always defined their role. What once unfolded inside kitchens now plays out before hundreds of onlookers.

Once the Namahage reach the shrine, they circle the great bonfire. The flames roar upward, sparks whirling into the night sky. The drumming grows louder, matched by the clanging of handbells. The figures dance in heavy, stamping steps, brandishing knives or pales (oke), shouting phrases that recall their admonitions in homes. The effect is theatrical, even celebratory, rather than frightening. Instead of cornering a child and demanding obedience, they now face the crowd as performers, moving in rhythm with the music. Their menace is stylized, controlled, and framed as entertainment.

This shift in tone is central to the festival's function. The household ritual relies on confrontation and fear: the shock of strangers in demon masks bursting into one's private space. The festival, by contrast, relies on spectacle and display: the awe of seeing costumed figures illuminated by bonfire and drums. The former enforces social norms, the latter showcases cultural heritage. Both use the same costumes, but the meaning is altered by context. In one setting the Namahage police behavior, in the other they affirm identity.

Throughout the festival, there are performances designed to involve the crowd. Small offerings of mochi are distributed after the Namahage complete their dance, symbolizing good fortune for the year ahead. Tourists line up to pose for photographs with the masked figures. Vendors sell hot drinks and local specialties. Souvenir stalls display miniature masks, keychains, and prints. The entire atmosphere resembles a winter fair, with the Namahage as its centerpiece. This is not accidental. The festival was conceived as a way to ensure the tradition would not fade and to attract visitors during Akita's long, difficult winters. It succeeds at both, but it also transforms the ritual into something new.

The Sedo Festival has become an important element of local identity. For residents of Oga, it provides a chance to present their heritage proudly to outsiders. School groups attend, local businesses benefit, and the municipality highlights the festival in promotional materials. The Namahage that once roared through village kitchens are now cultural ambassadors, representing Akita to the world. This shift parallels the broader trajectory of many folk traditions in Japan, where regional rituals have been reinterpreted as expressions of national heritage.

Yet the festival also raises questions about authenticity. Can a ritual retain its meaning when removed from the household and placed on a stage? Some local elders argue that the festival version lacks the raw power of the original, that tourists who clap and cheer cannot grasp the weight of the demon's questions. Others counter that without such public visibility, the Namahage might have disappeared entirely in the face of depopulation and modern skepticism. For many, the festival and the household visits are two sides of the same coin: one sustains community memory, the other ensures survival in a global age.

Comparisons with similar transformations elsewhere underscore the point. The Alpine Krampus has become a tourist parade, drawing photographers and foreign visitors, yet still carries fear for local children in private encounters. The Kukeri of Bulgaria now march through choreographed festivals, but their roots in agricultural purification remain recognized. In each case, the ritual adapts by moving from intimate space to public spectacle, from discipline to performance. The Sedo Festival belongs to this pattern, but what sets it apart is the coexistence of both forms. The Namahage are still alive in kitchens on December 31, even as they dance before bonfires in February.

For visitors, the Sedo Festival provides a rare chance to witness something both ancient and staged. They experience a distillation of the Namahage tradition, packaged for public consumption but still connected to local belief. For locals, the festival serves as both economic resource and cultural anchor. Its success has ensured municipal and national support, culminating in UNESCO recognition. But for the Namahage themselves, as figures of fear and admonition, the festival is a kind of translation. They speak a new language now, one shaped by cameras, applause, and international attention. The household ritual may terrify a child, but the festival ritual reassures the world that the Namahage are still here.

The Sedo Festival is therefore more than an entertainment. It is a negotiation between past and present, private ritual and public performance, fear and celebration. In the firelit faces of the Namahage, spectators see both the remnants of a demon who once judged them in the dark of their homes and the emblem of a culture determined to survive. The tension between these two roles will shape the future of the tradition. Whether the Namahage endure as living fear or as cultural icon may depend on how well this balance is maintained.

Section 3: UNESCO and the Language of Heritage

In December 2018, the Namahage were inscribed on UNESCO's Representative List of the Intangible Cultural Heritage of Humanity. The listing did not single out Oga alone but grouped the Namahage with nine other "Raiho-shin" traditions of visiting deities and demons across Japan, from Kagoshima's Toshidon to Noto's Amamehagi. Together they were recognized as expressions of Japan's winter visitation rites, a category of practices in which masked figures cross into communities to admonish, bless, or purify. For Oga, the UNESCO designation represented a moment of international validation, securing the Namahage's place on a global stage.

The decision carried both practical and symbolic consequences. On the practical side, UNESCO recognition opens channels for funding, preservation programs, and cultural exchange. It guarantees that the Namahage will be treated as national treasures, eligible for protection and promotion through both government and non-government institutions. For local organizers, it brings prestige and the promise of increased tourism.

The Namahage Museum and Oga's municipal government quickly highlighted the designation in promotional campaigns. Posters and brochures began to announce Oga as home to a world-recognized tradition, encouraging visitors to witness the demons firsthand.

On the symbolic side, the designation marks a shift in how the ritual is understood. What was once an intimate household event, carried out by neighbors in the shadows of snowbound villages, has been reframed as "heritage." In UNESCO's language, the Namahage are not merely local demons but representatives of humanity's cultural diversity. This confers legitimacy but also imposes a certain interpretation. Heritage must be preserved, cataloged, and displayed. The Namahage are thus placed in the same category as the flamenco of Spain, the samba of Brazil, and the carnival traditions of Europe. Their survival is no longer only a matter for Oga's villagers but a responsibility recognized by the international community.

The paradox is clear. UNESCO recognition safeguards the Namahage by ensuring that their tradition cannot be easily dismissed or forgotten. Yet the very act of preservation risks freezing the ritual into a static form. A living practice that once evolved organically, adapting to the needs of each household and generation, now finds itself described in official documents and staged for observers. The UNESCO dossier speaks of "visiting deities" and "ritual admonition," abstracting the demons into cultural symbols. While accurate, such language strips away the immediacy of the experience, the trembling child and the booming voice at the door.

This tension is not unique to Oga. Across the world, communities whose practices are inscribed on UNESCO's list find themselves negotiating between vitality and preservation. In some cases, listing has revitalized fading traditions, providing resources for transmission to younger generations. In others, it has led to a kind of museumification, where the practice is maintained for demonstration rather than lived belief. The Namahage sit uneasily between these two outcomes. The household visits still continue, though fewer families participate each year. At the same time, the Sedo Festival grows in scale, drawing thousands of visitors. The UNESCO designation supports the latter more easily than the former, since festivals can be scheduled, advertised, and staged, while intimate house visits resist such visibility.

Local voices reflect this ambivalence. Some residents express pride that their demons now stand alongside global icons of culture, confident that the recognition will draw young people back to a region suffering from depopulation. Others worry that the Namahage have been taken out of their context, turned into heritage objects for tourists rather than agents of communal discipline. For them, UNESCO's embrace is double-edged: it honors the tradition but alters its meaning. Once a figure that burst into homes to demand obedience, the Namahage is now celebrated as a bearer of cultural diversity.

Still, the inscription has ensured that the Namahage will not vanish quietly. By linking them to a broader family of Raiho-shin rituals, UNESCO has reinforced the idea that the Namahage are not isolated curiosities but part of a larger human pattern. The act of recognition situates Oga's demons within a global conversation about why communities invent and maintain rituals of fear. In this sense, UNESCO has amplified the very themes that give the Namahage their intellectual resonance. The demons at the door now stand as representatives not only of Oga but of the enduring human need for ritualized confrontation.

The question remains how the balance will be managed. Will the UNESCO designation preserve the Namahage as a living ritual, or transform them into a staged performance, polished for international visitors? The answer likely lies in whether the household visits continue. As long as villagers open their doors on December 31 and allow the figures to enter, the Namahage will remain more than heritage. They will remain fear embodied, not simply symbol displayed.

The Sedo Festival and the UNESCO listing may protect the image, but only the homes of Oga can protect the reality.

Section 4: Commodification and Community

The Namahage who once arrived only at the doors of Oga's households now circulate in a wider world. They descend mountains for tourists, appear on posters in railway stations, peer from souvenir shelves, and stride across the pages of manga. Their voice still echoes in kitchens each December, but their face has been translated into dozens of new settings. To understand what the Namahage mean today, one must follow them across these arenas: into the shops and festivals where they are commodified, into the media where they are reinvented as icons, and finally into the paradoxical space where ritual, performance, and image coexist.

In Oga, it is almost impossible to avoid the Namahage's image. At the Namahage Museum, a visitor can buy miniature wooden masks, each hand-painted in bright colors. At roadside stations, children's toys dressed in straw cloaks dangle from racks, their horns softened into rounded caricatures. Bottles of sake are labeled with snarling demon faces, as if the drink carries the same fire that once roared in kitchens. Even the local bus system uses stylized Namahage as a logo, turning demons into guides for travelers.

This saturation is not simply commercial opportunism. For rural Akita, the Namahage have become a lifeline. The prefecture faces severe depopulation, with shrinking villages and aging populations. Tourism is one of the few strategies available for economic revival, and the Namahage provide a brand unlike any other. Unlike invented mascots that dot the Japanese landscape, the Namahage rest on a genuine ritual with centuries of history. By foregrounding this tradition, Oga can distinguish itself from countless other struggling towns.

Municipal promotion reflects this strategy clearly. Posters in Tokyo stations depict towering straw-cloaked figures against snowy backdrops, urging urban residents to visit Akita's winter festivals. Pamphlets highlight the Namahage not only as folklore but as evidence of living heritage, borrowing the language of UNESCO recognition. Seasonal campaigns position Oga as "the land of the Namahage," anchoring regional identity in the demon's face. The commodified image functions as both advertisement and promise: here is a place where the old still lives.

Yet for local residents, the commodification is more complicated. Older villagers sometimes complain that the mask has been made to smile, its fierce lines softened into rounded mascots. They remember nights of childhood terror when the Namahage burst through doors, demanding obedience. To see that demon now dancing across candy wrappers feels to them like a betrayal. Others, however, express pride. For them, the spread of the Namahage's image is proof that their home has achieved recognition. Without such visibility, the ritual might fade unnoticed, another casualty of rural decline.

Both views capture the paradox of commodification. On the one hand, it erodes the aura of fear, translating demons into mascots. On the other, it ensures survival, embedding the figure in everyday life and economic circulation. A mask that roars only once a year may vanish; a mask that smiles daily from posters cannot be forgotten.

This dynamic is not unique to Oga. Across Japan, regional mascots, known as yuru-kyara, have become vehicles for local identity. From Kumamon the bear in Kumamoto to Hikonyan the armored cat in Shiga, communities market themselves through approachable characters. The Namahage fit awkwardly into this genre. They are not inventions of the last decade but figures rooted in lived fear. To place them alongside cartoon cats and bears risks trivialization. Yet refusing the mascot logic would mean declining the economic benefits that such branding brings. Oga's strategy has been to do both: retain the terrifying ritual while circulating softened images for public consumption.

In practice, the two forms are not equal. Tourists may buy a keychain or pose with a costumed Namahage at the Sedo Festival, but only a shrinking number of families still open their doors on December 31. The commodified image thrives, while the embodied encounter struggles. Preservationists argue that without the income generated by tourism and souvenirs, even the household ritual would be endangered. Critics respond that a figure transformed into merchandise loses its soul. The debate continues, but the reality is clear: commodification has become one of the pillars supporting the Namahage's endurance.

Section 5: Namahage as Icon

Beyond commerce, the Namahage have entered the realm of popular culture and media. Their horned faces appear in anime series that gather yokai into fantastical storylines. Manga artists sketch them as part of rural landscapes, sometimes accurately rendered with straw cloaks, other times distorted into more generic demons. In video games, they serve as monsters to be fought, names attached to designs that bear little resemblance to the Oga originals. In these forms, the Namahage move far from their home, becoming part of a global circulation of folkloric figures.

The effect is double-edged. For many consumers, the Namahage encountered in a game or comic are interchangeable with other demons. The specificity of the ritual, the stern questioning of children, the snowbound villages of Akita, vanish into the background. What remains is the horned mask, the label of "Japanese demon." The figure is flattened into archetype. Yet these appearances also extend reach. Someone who first meets a Namahage on a screen may later learn of Oga and its traditions. Media appearances keep the figure alive in the cultural imagination, ensuring that it does not sink into obscurity.

Tourism campaigns amplify this process. National and international posters feature the Namahage in bold silhouettes, often against snowy backdrops or fiery festival scenes. Design choices vary: some emphasize menace, others playfully stylize the mask into approachable shapes. In each case, the figure becomes a symbol of regional identity. The demon who once terrified children is now an ambassador for Akita Prefecture, appearing on billboards, pamphlets, and even airline advertisements.

Graphic design further transforms the figure. The sharp horns and glaring eyes are softened into rounded forms suitable for children's coloring books or festival balloons. These versions bear little resemblance to the towering straw-cloaked figures who demand obedience in darkened kitchens. Yet they circulate widely, reaching audiences far removed from Oga. The demon becomes familiar, even friendly.

For residents, this dual life provokes reflection. Some embrace the media presence as proof that their tradition matters beyond their village. Others worry that being reduced to an icon strips the Namahage of their function as disciplinarian. Both views are valid, for both processes are real.

The mask terrifies fewer children each year, but it inspires recognition across Japan and beyond.

Section 6: Closing Reflection

The story of the Namahage today is therefore not a single narrative but a layered coexistence. In homes on New Year's Eve, they still roar questions and instill fear. In February, they perform before bonfires, celebrated as cultural heritage. Year-round, they smile from souvenirs, appear in media, and function as icons of Akita identity. Each setting alters their meaning, but together they sustain their survival.

The paradox is unavoidable. A demon no one recognizes will vanish. A demon everyone laughs at will lose its power. The Namahage endure by moving between registers, frightening in kitchens, entertaining at festivals, reassuring on posters. They are both demon and mascot, both heritage and brand. This mobility is the price of endurance in a modern world.

For scholars and residents alike, the question is not whether the Namahage are "authentic" in one form or another. It is how the tradition negotiates these transformations, and whether the core of embodied discipline, the reminder that laziness, disobedience, and neglect carry consequences, can survive amidst souvenirs and media icons. As long as families still open their doors on December 31, the answer remains yes. The ritual continues, even if reframed.

The next chapter turns from institutions, festivals, and images to voices. What do the people of Oga themselves say about their demons? How do they recall the terror of childhood visits, and how do they interpret the tourist spectacles and commodified masks that surround them now? To understand the Namahage fully, one must listen not only to the roar of the demon but also to the reflections of those who live with it year after year.

CHAPTER 12: Ethnographic Voices

Section 1: Early Ethnographers and Folklorists

When the Namahage first attracted the attention of folklorists in the early twentieth century, they were not treated as local curiosities but as windows into the deep structure of Japanese belief. Intellectuals of the Meiji and Taishō eras were eager to catalog the remnants of what they imagined as an older, purer Japan, a body of custom uncorrupted by Westernization and modernization. To them, the horned visitors of Oga represented not only the eccentricity of a snowbound peninsula but the survival of an archaic logic in which gods, demons, and humans intermingled at the threshold.

A key voice in this early folklore turn was Yanagita Kunio (1875–1962), often described as a founder of minzokugaku. Though he did not carry out sustained fieldwork in Oga, his national framework influenced how observers read rites like the Namahage, as residues of agrarian religious patterns rather than mere local mumming. In Yanagita's account, midwinter house-visits could echo the toshigami, New Year deities thought to descend to inspect and renew households; the noisy intrusion at the door could thus be read as a later, roughened fragment of older divine visitation. This perspective helped place the Namahage within a broader rural religious lexicon without asserting an unbroken line to antiquity.

Orikuchi Shinobu, Yanagita's student and a poet-scholar, extended the visitation thesis. In essays on year's-end observances he posited a class of **raihō-shin**—"visiting deities"—who cross from the other world at calendrical thresholds to receive hospitality, inspect conduct, and confer protection. He set the Oga figures within this continuum: their New Year timing, demand for offerings, and ritual scolding read as survivals of divine inspection. The jagged mask and demonic bravado, in his view, were later theatrical layers laid over an older cult of welcoming the **toshigami**. What endures is the logic of visitation: a god arrives, the household answers, and the year is secured.

This mythological reading proved durable. It reassured urban intellectuals that the countryside still carried traces of an ancient, sacred order. It also softened the roughness of the practice. What might otherwise appear to be parents terrifying their children was reinterpreted as a degraded form of divine visitation. This interpretive move was not neutral. It elevated the Namahage from a local custom to part of the national heritage of belief, aligning them with broader narratives of Japanese spirituality.

At the same time, many early accounts reveal their distance from lived experience, describing Namahage in abstract terms, as survivals or archetypes, rather than as events that left children screaming under futons. They were fascinated by the figure as symbol but less attentive to the emotion it generated in real households. The voices of villagers themselves appear only in fragments, usually as evidence to support theoretical claims.

By the 1920s and 1930s, field surveys conducted by local historians and folklorists began to gather more concrete detail. Reports described the costumes in precise terms, the straw cloaks, the carved masks, the bundles of knives or buckets carried in hand. They noted the timing of the ritual on New Year's Eve, the questions asked of children, the role of parents in responding to the demons' accusations. These accounts laid the groundwork for later, more anthropological analyses. Yet they still tended to frame the Namahage as relics of an earlier, premodern Japan rather than as dynamic practices embedded in living communities.

One theme that emerges consistently from early accounts is the moralizing function of the Namahage. Writers observed that the demons asked whether children had been lazy or disobedient, and interpreted this as a direct tool of social discipline. They contrasted the Namahage with Western traditions like Santa Claus, noting that where the foreign figure rewarded good behavior with gifts, the Japanese figure punished bad behavior with threats. This comparison was sometimes framed in nationalist terms, as evidence of Japan's distinct cultural emphasis on shame, responsibility, and communal discipline. However, that tidy opposition overlooks other winter figures who admonish or punish, Krampus in Alpine regions, Père Fouettard in France, Belsnickel in the Rhineland diaspora. Likewise, Namahage nights braid rebuke with thanks, sake, and renewal. The more accurate distinction isn't between cultures, but in how each community calibrates warning and blessing to its own aims and conditions.

It is important to recognize how the context of the early twentieth century shaped these interpretations. Japan was undergoing rapid modernization and Westernization. Intellectuals were anxious to assert the uniqueness of Japanese culture while also demonstrating that it contained universal patterns recognizable to comparative folklore. The Namahage provided a convenient case: simultaneously exotic and familiar, terrifying and instructive, archaic yet alive. Scholars could present the ritual as evidence that Japan retained a living connection to its mythic past even as it raced toward modernity.

For contemporary readers, these early accounts are invaluable but partial. They preserve descriptions of practices that might otherwise have been lost. They also reveal the interpretive frameworks of their time, frameworks that emphasized continuity with ancient gods, celebrated the moralizing power of shame, and often ignored the voices of the villagers themselves. They show us how the Namahage were understood by the intellectual class long before the rise of mass tourism or UNESCO recognition.

Perhaps most striking is the contrast between the cosmic scale of interpretation offered by Yanagita and Orikuchi and the domestic scale of the ritual itself. To the villagers of Oga, the Namahage were immediate and visceral: masked figures demanding answers in a kitchen on a snowy night. To the folklorists, they were survivals of myth, echoes of deities, fragments of an ancient worldview. Both perspectives are true in their own way, but they operate on different registers. The task of later anthropologists and ethnographers would be to bring these registers together, situating the symbolic within the lived, and giving equal weight to the terror of a child's memory and the theoretical elegance of mythological continuity.

Section 2: Postwar Anthropologists and Observers

In the decades after the war, the study of Namahage shifted from grand theories of mythic survivals to closer attention to lived practice. Researchers arrived in Oga with notebooks, tape recorders, and cameras, prepared to sit on cold floors with families, to follow costumed men through snowed-in lanes, and to ask what the ritual felt like from the inside. The emphasis moved toward description and toward the micropolitics of the visit itself, the choreography of who speaks when, who laughs, who cries, and who decides the scene has gone far enough.

Fieldworkers in the 1950s and 1960s were struck first by the density of collaboration that lies behind the appearance of chaos. The demon at the door looks like an intruder, yet the visit is made possible by a network of permissions. Mothers usher children into the main room, fathers or uncles quietly check that the hearth is safe and that fragile objects are out of reach, neighbors confirm which households will receive a visit. The moment of alarm is built on a scaffolding of consent, and this paradox became a central theme in postwar accounts. What looks like a breach is in fact a carefully managed opening in the social fabric, a permitted transgression whose limits are known to all.

Researchers also documented the standard beats of the script. There is the knock or the sudden entrance, the booming voice that calls the names of disobedient children, the ritual questions about study, chores, and obedience, the parent who bargains on a child's behalf, the promise of reform, and the eventual withdrawal of the visitors. Within this pattern, field notes record variations that reveal the flexibility of the rite. Some demons tease before they scold, others go straight to accusation. In certain neighborhoods the men carry wooden knives and ladles, in others they lift the straw of their cloaks high above their heads to amplify their size. The frame is shared, the performance is local.

Attention to children's experience sharpened as anthropologists took testimony from multiple age groups. Adults remembered the event as a lesson, a turning point in a winter of idleness that jolted them back to effort. Children described the same night as a maze of sensation, the heat of the hearth, the smell of damp straw, the crack of the voice that seemed not to belong to any human they knew. Many reported the same sequence of emotions, terror while it happened, relief as the masks retreated, and a dawning pride that they had endured. Postwar accounts showed how memory edits the experience, converting fear into a story of belonging, and how families retell the visit in later weeks to reinforce promises made at the door.

Scholars used these descriptions to test larger ideas about ritual and socialization. Some argued that Namahage functions as a controlled ordeal that moves children across a seasonal threshold, from winter slackness to the obligations of the new year. Others explored how the visit externalizes surveillance, making communal judgment visible through a body that is both familiar and strange. The conversation about shame and guilt cultures, which was widespread in mid-century social science, inevitably touched the Namahage. Careful ethnography complicated simple contrasts. The rite uses shame, since the child is named publicly and measured against communal standards, but it also induces inward reckoning, the kind of self-assessment that carries over when the masks are gone.

Family dynamics received sustained attention. Observers noted the triad that structures the scene, the child as subject, the demon as accuser, the parent as mediator and interpreter. Parents sometimes conspired to heighten the drama, preparing specific criticisms for the visitors to voice. In other homes, adults softened the encounter, stepping forward early to promise improvement and to signal that enough had been said. This plasticity, recorded across neighborhoods and years, convinced many researchers that the Namahage are not a blunt instrument of social control but a flexible medium for negotiating expectations, with parents using the figure to say what they cannot easily say in their own voices.

Accounts of performers themselves added another layer. Men who wore the masks described the experience as exhausting and exhilarating. They spoke of the weight of the straw and the heat of the room, of the effort required to keep the voice low and impersonal, of the temptation to break character when a child they knew began to sob. Several admitted that the mask grants a peculiar freedom. Behind it they could speak with a severity they would avoid in everyday life, and they could direct that speech toward adults as well as children. Postwar writers seized on this testimony to argue that the Namahage dramatize a temporary redistribution of authority. Authority leaves the recognizable faces of the village and reappears in a form that is not accountable to ordinary politeness, which allows certain truths to be said.

A smaller body of postwar work tracked the rite across the yearly cycle and across the local economy. Researchers looked at how men balanced preparation for the visit with winter fishing, snow clearing, and shrine obligations. They recorded the practical labor of making and repairing straw cloaks, the sourcing of wood for masks, and the quiet prestige that attaches to households that maintain the craft. These studies insisted that the Namahage cannot be isolated from other forms of communal cooperation. The visit crowns a season of shared work, and the memory of it is folded back into that same network of mutual aid.

By the late Shōwa period, depopulation and the growth of the Sedo Festival had begun to shape ethnographic questions. Fieldworkers asked whether the presence of visitors with cameras influenced how the masks moved through streets or how long they lingered in each home. They noted that some families declined visits, citing young children or elderly relatives, and they tracked the way neighborhood routes were adjusted year by year. The ritual was still private at its core, yet it was increasingly performed with an awareness that it existed in a broader field of representation. Researchers were attentive to the quiet negotiations that keep the household rite intact, even as the public festival drew attention outward.

Postwar observers also refined the language used to describe what the Namahage do to a room. Rather than speak only of fear, they wrote in terms of intensity and attentiveness. When the masks enter, time thickens, and bodies reorient around the figures. Children are brought to the center, adults take up positions at the edges, the chimney smoke seems to slow, and even the dogs fall silent. The scene acquires a density that ordinary scolding cannot achieve. The description is not romantic. It is a way of marking how a community creates a heightened moment in which speech lands differently and promises carry unusual weight.

If early folklorists treated the Namahage as survivals of gods, postwar anthropologists treated them as instruments of social life, devices through which families speak to one another across a boundary of costume and voice. The shift did not deny the sacred register that older writers heard. It translated that register into observable forms, the itinerary of a night, the shaping of a room, the uses of a mask.

This attention to practice opens naturally toward the next section, where the voices of Oga residents speak at length about what they remember and how their understanding has changed across generations.

Section 3: Oral Histories from Oga Residents

If scholars mapped the Namahage as gods or as instruments of social order, residents of Oga remember them in the grain of experience: the sound of straw scraping against wooden floors, the rush of cold air as the door swung wide, the weight of a hand that smelled of smoke and sweat. Oral histories collected from the peninsula in the late twentieth and early twenty-first centuries reveal a spectrum of emotions that no theory can fully capture. To listen to villagers speak of their childhood encounters is to enter the world where the ritual lived most vividly.

Elderly residents recall the Namahage of the 1940s and 1950s as overwhelming, almost elemental. A woman born in 1943 described hiding beneath the heavy quilt of the kotatsu, trembling as horns and straw filled the doorway. She remembered her father stepping aside, letting the demon approach, while her mother tried to soothe her with whispers. "I knew it was my uncle," she said, "but in that moment I could not believe it. The voice was too large, the mask too cruel." The memory carried both fear and recognition: terror at the figure itself, and later amusement that she had been taken in by someone so familiar.

Others recall the way the Namahage's questions cut to the core of childhood anxieties. Men who grew up in fishing households speak of being asked whether they had shirked helping with nets, or whether they had wasted rice. Students were asked if they had been diligent in study. The questions were tailored, and children understood them as indictments of their specific failings. One man remembered the sting of being accused of laziness when his schoolwork had indeed lapsed. The shame burned, he said, "more than the stick." Yet he also admitted that the accusation spurred him to improve, so that when the Namahage came the following year he could meet them with pride.

Children sometimes resisted. Several narrators described fighting the impulse to cry, trying to show courage in front of siblings or cousins. One woman remembered her older brother vowing to stare the mask down, only to burst into tears when the demon lifted him bodily off the floor. The moment became a family anecdote, retold at gatherings, both mocking and affectionate. Oral history reveals how these scenes are not only lived but replayed in memory, woven into the family's collective narrative. The Namahage visit becomes a story about the child's temperament, one repeated for decades afterward.

Parents also appear in these memories, sometimes as allies, sometimes as co-conspirators. Many narrators spoke of the shock of realizing in adulthood that their mother or father had arranged the accusations, whispering to the masked visitors which faults to highlight. Betrayal was one word that recurred in recollection, but so did gratitude. Several villagers said they understood only later that the ruse allowed their parents to scold them through another voice, to say things they could not bear to say directly. A daughter recalled that her mother asked the Namahage to warn her against wandering too far into the snow. Only later did she realize that the mask was her mother's way of expressing deep fear for her safety.

Generational differences mark these accounts. Older villagers remember a Namahage who entered without hesitation, overturning furniture, scattering ash, frightening even adults. Middle-aged residents recall more controlled encounters, with demons who kept to a script and avoided excessive chaos. The shift reflects a slow moderation of the ritual, as households adapted to modern sensibilities and to the presence of outsiders. Oral history captures this change not as abstract decline but as lived contrast: "When I was young, they were wild," said one man in his sixties, "but when my children were small, the Namahage had already learned to smile."

The pride of having been visited also surfaces repeatedly. Adults look back on their childhood fear as proof of membership in a community that values discipline and endurance. To be chased, scolded, or dragged by the wrist was to be included in a drama that bound neighbors together. A man who left Oga for work in Tokyo spoke of telling his colleagues about the Namahage and finding that none had anything similar. His childhood shame became in retrospect a badge of distinction. "It meant we belonged to a place that had not forgotten itself," he said. Oral history reveals how terror is reframed over time as honor, the sting of accusation converted into the glow of identity.

Not all memories are positive. Some narrators spoke of lasting scars. A woman recalled that her younger sister was so terrified she developed a fever the following day. Others mentioned children who refused to eat or who wet their beds after the visit. These accounts complicate any romantic picture of the Namahage as harmless theatrics. They underscore the real psychological force the ritual exerted, force that could tip into trauma. Residents acknowledge this risk, even as most frame it as part of the rite's seriousness. "It was not meant to be gentle," one said. "It was meant to mark you."

Recent oral testimonies highlight a tension between continuity and performance. Many who grew up in the 1990s–2000s encountered the Namahage both at home and in staged festival settings, recognized the same masks on television, posters, and keychains, and even watched costuming demonstrations at the Namahage Museum (Namahage-kan); for them, the fear is rarely absolute. Yet they still describe a persistent charge at the threshold: even knowing the figures are neighbors and the event is performative, the encounter tightens the stomach and briefly restores the weight of the older terror.

These testimonies reveal how the Namahage function across the life course. As children, villagers experienced them as terrifying others. As adults, they interpret them as pedagogical tools, family dramas, and sources of pride. For emigrants, they become markers of origin, stories to tell in distant cities. For the elderly, they are signs of a world that is fading, yet still present each winter. Oral history thus complements ethnography: where field notes capture the structure of the visit, memory records its emotional afterlife.

Together they show that the Namahage are not only a ritual event but a thread of narrative that runs through an entire life, resurfacing at kitchen tables decades later, reshaped by nostalgia, humor, or regret.

Section 4: Contemporary Voices and Tensions

If memories of the mid-century Namahage are steeped in fear and later pride, contemporary voices reveal a more ambivalent landscape. The ritual survives, but its meaning has been reframed by demographic decline, by tourism, and by the global reach of Japanese cultural branding. Interviews and local surveys from the past two decades show that Oga residents navigate the Namahage today with mixed feelings: gratitude for the attention it brings, anxiety about its dilution, and uncertainty about whether the rite can still serve its original disciplinary purpose.

The most striking shift is generational. Children growing up in Oga in the 1990s and 2000s often experienced the Namahage not as a singular ordeal but as one event among many winter entertainments. They were as likely to see the figures at the Sedo Festival or on a school field trip to the Namahage Museum as in the dim room of their family's home. For some, this familiarity blunted the shock. A boy interviewed in 2008 admitted that he laughed when the mask entered because he recognized his neighbor's boots under the straw. Yet he still described the atmosphere as "serious," because adults treated the questions with gravity. The fear was lighter, but the ritual still produced a moment of heightened attention.

Teenagers express more skepticism. Several said they regarded the Namahage as "for the tourists," a performance staged for outsiders rather than an inner necessity of village life. One high school student in 2016 remarked, "It is something we show, not something we believe." Yet in the same conversation she acknowledged that she would not want the ritual to end, because it marked Oga as different from other towns. The contradiction is telling. Even when belief fades, attachment remains, reconstituted as pride in local distinctiveness.

For parents, the question is practical as well as symbolic. Some still arrange for visits, whispering complaints to the costumed men, eager for the discipline that a mask can deliver more effectively than parental nagging. Others decline, worried that the shock may be too intense for very young children, or that neighbors may judge them for clinging to outdated practices. The decision has become optional, no longer an automatic part of the New Year's cycle. Oral testimony suggests that this very optionality changes the meaning: a visit is now a choice rather than a given, an event selected to affirm identity as much as to enforce discipline.

Local organizers, especially those involved in the Sedo Festival, emphasize the need to balance tradition with spectacle. They are aware that large crowds come less to see authentic household visits than to witness dozens of straw-cloaked figures dancing before bonfires. Organizers speak of the responsibility to present the Namahage as both terrifying and approachable, something children can fear but tourists can photograph. This balancing act produces ambivalence. On the one hand, the festival generates income, visibility, and official recognition. On the other, it threatens to reduce the Namahage to theater, detaching the mask from the intimate household drama that gave it force.

The 2018 UNESCO inscription of "Raiho-shin, ritual visits of deities in masks and costumes"—a nationwide listing that includes Oga's Namahage, deepened these tensions. Some residents celebrated the designation as an honor that guaranteed survival. Others voiced suspicion, wondering whether heritage status would turn the ritual into a fossil, preserved for outsiders but drained of local vitality. A fisherman in his fifties remarked, "If UNESCO protects it, that is good, but who will protect the feeling of children when the demon enters? No committee can do that." His words capture the dilemma: external recognition may ensure continuity, but it cannot manufacture the trembling silence of a room when horns cross the threshold.

Economic realities reinforce the stakes. Akita's shrinking population means fewer families to host visits and fewer young men to don the straw. Organizers worry about recruitment, about whether enough volunteers will be willing to endure the physical burden of the costume. Some have experimented with training programs, inviting younger participants to practice in safer settings before entering homes. This professionalization signals both dedication and fragility: the Namahage must now be cultivated deliberately, not simply inherited as a matter of course.

There is also the question of how outsiders perceive the ritual. Tourists often describe the Namahage in terms of charm and excitement, praising the spectacle without engaging its harsher undertones. Residents notice this difference. They remark that visitors clap and cheer at the Sedo Festival, but in the home the silence is heavier, punctured only by a child's sob. Some locals express relief that outsiders cannot see the full severity of the visit, which might invite criticism. Others worry that if the ritual is only known through festival performances, its moral dimension will vanish entirely.

Contemporary voices thus oscillate between pride and anxiety. Many residents take satisfaction in seeing the Namahage on posters, in anime, and in travel brochures. They know that without this circulation, Oga would be one more name in the long list of depopulating coastal towns. Yet they also guard the memory of private nights when fear was sharp, and they lament that such nights are fewer each year. The Namahage are sustained by visibility, but their meaning depends on intimacy.

Balancing the two has become the central challenge of the present era.

What emerges from these testimonies is not a consensus but a mosaic of perspectives. Children giggle, parents calculate, organizers strategize, elders recall, and officials promote. The Namahage inhabit all these registers at once. To reduce them to heritage or to entertainment alone is to miss the complexity of a figure that still knocks at doors while also smiling from souvenirs.

The voices of today's Oga remind us that rituals do not survive in the abstract. They endure only insofar as people decide, year after year, to open the door, to let the demons in, and to accept the ambivalence that follows.

Section 5: Outsider vs. Insider Perspectives

The ethnographic record of the Namahage is, in many ways, a dialogue between two vantage points: that of outsiders who arrive with notebooks, cameras, or expectations of spectacle, and that of insiders whose lives have been shaped by the yearly visitation. The contrast between the two perspectives is not absolute, since villagers sometimes adopt the language of tourism and scholars sometimes glimpse the intimacy of fear. But the tension remains instructive, because it highlights how meaning shifts depending on who is speaking and for whom the story is told.

Outsiders have often described the Namahage in terms of archetype and symbol. The folklorists of the early twentieth century framed them as remnants of gods, survivals of archaic belief. Postwar anthropologists read them as instruments of socialization, situating them within debates about shame and community. Tourists, in turn, write in diaries and travelogues about "terrifying but fascinating demons," cataloging the color of the masks or the drama of the Sedo Festival. In each case the Namahage appear as objects of analysis or entertainment, figures to be categorized or consumed. The emphasis falls on the visible, mask, straw, horn, knife, and on the general patterns they illustrate. Outsider voices speak of what the Namahage represent.

Insiders speak differently. Oral histories reveal less concern with symbolism and more with sensation: the smell of straw, the heat of the fire, the thud of a hand on the floorboards. They recall embarrassment when named in front of siblings, the laughter that followed tears, the pride of survival. Insiders describe not what the Namahage mean but what they do. The figure is not a type or a symbol but an experience that rearranges the room and leaves a mark on memory. Outsider and insider voices cross in places, but their emphases remain distinct, concept versus impact, abstraction versus immediacy.

This divergence becomes especially clear when examining the notion of discipline. Outsiders often celebrate the Namahage as a device for social control, a picturesque example of how Japanese culture emphasizes shame over guilt. For villagers, discipline is less a theory than a practical effect. Parents recall relief that their children listened more attentively after a visit, that chores were taken up with greater seriousness. Children remember resolving to do better, not because they had reflected on cultural norms but because they had been startled into a promise. Outsider accounts elevate the practice into comparative anthropology; insider accounts present it as household management with teeth.

A similar divergence appears in responses to commodification. Outsiders are quick to note the irony of terrifying demons turned into plush dolls and bus logos. Scholars debate whether heritage status and festivalization dilute authenticity. Residents voice pride and worry in more entangled ways. They know that souvenirs sustain local shops, that visitors keep hotels open, that

UNESCO recognition brings attention. At the same time, they measure authenticity by whether the Namahage still enter homes. For them the line is not between pure ritual and corrupted performance but between the living knock on the door and the distant image on a poster. Outsider voices stress heritage; insider voices stress presence.

There are moments, however, when the perspectives converge. Some tourists who have been invited into private homes write with awe at the silence that falls when the mask appears, echoing insider accounts of intensity. Some villagers adopt the language of symbolism when explaining the custom to journalists, speaking of "discipline" and "tradition" rather than of fear and tears. The two perspectives bleed into one another, shaped by encounters and expectations. Yet the differences remain crucial, because they show how the Namahage contain multiple layers of meaning simultaneously.

Anthropologists have sometimes framed this as a question of audience. For whom is the performance staged? When it is for children, the aim is transformation through fear. When it is for tourists, the aim is spectacle and education. When it is for scholars, the aim is explanation. Each audience elicits a different Namahage, and each Namahage is real in its own frame. What oral histories demonstrate is that villagers are acutely aware of these shifting audiences. They can joke about the tourist-friendly demon while still trembling at the memory of the household visit. Outsider accounts may privilege one register, but insiders inhabit all at once.

The interplay of outsider and insider perspectives underscores a central anthropological lesson: rituals are not static objects to be cataloged but dynamic events whose meaning depends on context, participant, and audience. The Namahage are especially revealing because they straddle so many boundaries, demon and god, discipline and entertainment, local identity and national symbol. Outsider voices chart these categories; insider voices feel their force. Together they produce a fuller portrait than either could alone.

As the Namahage continue to circulate in festivals, museums, and media, the distance between outsider and insider perspectives narrows in some respects and widens in others. Outsiders become more familiar with the imagery, sometimes flattening it into a brand. Insiders wrestle with whether to keep the household visits alive or to accept that public performances suffice. Both perspectives matter, and the friction between them is part of the ritual's contemporary life. To hear only one is to mistake the Namahage for either a quaint spectacle or a private terror. To hear both is to understand that the figure endures precisely because it can hold these contradictory meanings at once.

Section 6: Reflection and Transition

Across more than a century of description, the Namahage have been interpreted as gods, demons, disciplinary tools, cultural artifacts, heritage symbols, and tourist attractions. What emerges most clearly from the ethnographic voices is not a single meaning but a layered field of perspectives that refuse to collapse into one another. The ritual endures because it has always been capable of carrying these multiple registers at once.

The early folklorists heard in the Namahage the distant echo of divine visitors, proof that agrarian Japan still held traces of an archaic religious order. Postwar anthropologists looked instead at practice, mapping the ritual as a technology of socialization, a way of making shame visible and binding families into shared responsibility. Oral histories add still another dimension: the textures of memory, the heat of the room, the sting of being named, the laughter of survival. Contemporary testimonies reveal ambivalence, a balancing of pride and skepticism, attachment and doubt, as Oga navigates depopulation, UNESCO recognition, and the pressures of tourism.

Taken together, these voices show that the Namahage cannot be reduced to symbol or function alone. They are not only gods degraded into demons, nor only parents disguising their admonitions, nor only mascots rebranded for travelers. They are all of these at once, shifting in meaning depending on who speaks, when, and for what audience. The ethnographic record makes this multiplicity visible. It shows that the Namahage are not frozen relics but dynamic figures that live differently in scholarship, in memory, in performance, and in commerce.

The contrast between outsider and insider perspectives crystallizes this lesson. Outsiders describe the ritual in terms of abstraction, myth, social order, heritage. Insiders recall it in terms of sensation, fear, shame, laughter, pride. Each perspective is partial; together they form a composite that more closely resembles the truth. To understand the Namahage is to move between these registers, to recognize that theory and memory illuminate different aspects of the same encounter.

This recognition prepares the way for broader reflection. If the Namahage endure, it is not because they have one stable meaning but because they accommodate change while preserving intensity. A child who trembles in 1950, a tourist who photographs in 2000, a scholar who writes in 1920, all engage with the same figure, yet each encounter yields a different lesson. The Namahage are capacious enough to contain all of them.

In this sense, the ethnographic voices do more than document a local custom. They offer a method for thinking about ritual itself: as lived, remembered, performed, analyzed, and reframed across time. The Namahage are not unique in this respect, but they are unusually vivid in showing how a practice can survive precisely by refusing to be pinned down to one meaning.

The reflections that follow in Part V will draw out the implications of this lesson. They will ask what ritualized fear offers to human communities, why terror can be formative rather than destructive, and how masks at the door continue to remind us of our obligations. The ethnographic voices of Oga, with their mixture of awe, humor, pride, and unease, give us the raw material for that meditation. They remind us that behind every theory lies a trembling child, a conspiring parent, or a weary performer with straw on his shoulders. To listen to them is to see that the mask is never only symbol. It is always also experience.

CHAPTER 13: The Lasting Image

The snow falls thick in late December, softening the edges of fields and burying the narrow roads that wind through the Oga Peninsula. Houses crouch under its weight, their roofs sloping low, light seeping faintly through paper screens. On certain nights the silence is so complete that even the sea seems hushed, waves muffled beneath the snow-charged air. For centuries it was in this stillness that villagers heard the sudden sound of straw crunching, voices rising, horns and teeth filling the doorway. Each winter, fear and renewal arrived together, bound in the masks of the Namahage. The rhythm was steady, as certain as the snow itself. Time bent around the ritual, and the ritual in turn carried time forward, reminding each generation that the year could not turn without a reckoning.

There was a comfort in that continuity. Children grew, became parents, grew old, and still the demons came. The same questions were asked: Have you worked? Have you studied? Have you obeyed? And laughter eventually followed once the terror subsided. In Oga, where mountains hemmed in villages and winter pressed hard, the Namahage seemed eternal. They belonged to the season as surely as the snow did. The ritual's persistence was proof that the world could remain familiar even as lives passed through it.

Yet time does not stand still, even in the remotest corners. At first it was the railway, then the hum of electric wires, then the glow of televisions. Each carried voices from elsewhere, softening the sense that Oga was apart from the world. What had been preserved by isolation began to change under contact. In recent decades the change has quickened, no longer a trickle but a flood. Broadband lines run beneath the same roads that the straw-clad figures once trod. The glow in December homes is as likely to be the cold light of a screen as the warmth of a hearth. Children who once trembled at horns and straw cloaks now know the faces of monsters in games and movies streamed from far beyond Akita. The Namahage still come, but they arrive in houses already filled with other voices. The silence that once framed their power is crowded now with the endless hum of connection.

This change is not unique to Oga. All across rural Japan, the snowballing reach of the internet and the steady drift of people to cities have thinned the boundaries that once preserved local traditions. Isolation once worked like a greenhouse, sheltering fragile customs so they could flourish in their own conditions. Now every window is open, every child a citizen of a larger, noisier world. What once felt timeless reveals itself to be fragile. Continuity was never automatic; it depended on remoteness, on difficulty, on the slowness of change. In its absence, rituals must either transform or wither.

The Namahage have not disappeared. They stride through festival grounds, they glare from posters in train stations, they are printed on sake bottles and toy masks sold to travelers. Their faces have multiplied rather than diminished, but multiplied in new ways. The intimacy of the household visit is paired with the spectacle of performance for tourists. What was once frightening in the dim glow of a farmhouse lamp is now staged beneath floodlights, photographed, uploaded, circulated. In this sense the Namahage have crossed into a new form of endurance. They are no longer bound only to Oga's kitchens; they belong also to the restless, global tide of images that the internet carries.

The question is what such endurance means. Is the ritual hollowed by its proliferation, or strengthened by its survival in any form? The Namahage were once guardians of discipline in harsh conditions, figures who reminded children of the cost of idleness. Do they still guard anything when they appear on glossy posters or in manga panels? Or do they become something gentler, more forgiving, content to be symbols rather than threats? The truth may be that they have always contained both possibilities. Even in the past, fear softened into laughter, terror into memory. The demon was never only punishment but also protection, never only judgment but also blessing. Perhaps in their new forms the Namahage are less harsh, but no less enduring.

It is tempting to imagine the Namahage themselves judging this transformation. Would they rage against the intrusion of the internet, against the shrinking of villages and the loss of silence? Would they accuse parents of allowing their children to be distracted by glowing screens rather than taught the lessons of discipline? Or would they recognize that change itself is part of survival, that rituals must shift to remain alive? One can picture them pausing at the threshold, horns catching the lamplight, uncertain whether to accuse or to forgive. The answer is not given. It lingers in the space between roar and silence.

Outside, the snow continues to fall, untroubled by memory or change. It buries roads and fields alike, covering both the old silences and the new voices that have entered the houses. Whether the Namahage accuse or forgive, they remain part of this rhythm, arriving each winter as the snow does. In their faces we glimpse not only the weight of the past but the uncertainty of what lies ahead. And so the year turns, carried forward by fear, by memory, and by the questions that still echo in the night.

Selected Bibliography

Miyamoto, Tsuneichi. *Wasurerareta Nihonjin* 『忘れられた日本人』 [The Forgotten Japanese]. Tokyo: Iwanami Shoten, 1984. (Iwanami Bunko edition)

Orikuchi, Shinobu. *Kodai Kenkyū* 『古代研究』 [Studies of Antiquity]. Tokyo: Hakubunkan, 1930–1934. (Multiple vols.)

Yanagita, Kunio. *Tōno Monogatari* 『遠野物語』 [The Legends of Tōno]. Tokyo: Kōdansha Gakujutsu Bunko, 1991. (Originally published 1910)

Yanagita, Kunio. *Nihon no Nenjū Gyōji* 『日本の年中行事』 [Annual Customs of Japan]. Tokyo: Kōdansha Gakujutsu Bunko, 1978.

Turner, Victor. *The Ritual Process: Structure and Anti-Structure*. Ithaca, NY: Cornell University Press, 1969.

Geertz, Clifford. *The Interpretation of Cultures: Selected Essays*. New York: Basic Books, 1973.

Van Gennep, Arnold. *Les Rites de Passage*. Paris: Émile Nourry, 1909. English translation: *The Rites of Passage*. Translated by Monika B. Vizedom and Gabrielle L. Caffee. Chicago: University of Chicago Press, 1960.

Mori, Masahiro. "Bukimi no tani" 『不気味の谷』. *Energy* 7, no. 4 (1970): 33–35. English translation: "The Uncanny Valley." Translated by Karl F. MacDorman and Norri Kageki. *IEEE Spectrum*, June 12, 2012. https://spectrum.ieee.org/the-uncanny-valley

UNESCO. "Raiho-shin, Ritual Visits of Deities in Masks and Costumes." *Representative List of the Intangible Cultural Heritage of Humanity*. Inscribed 2018. https://ich.unesco.org/en/RL/raiho-shin-ritual-visits-of-deities-in-masks-and-costumes-01271.

Ministry of Foreign Affairs of Japan. "Inscription of 'Raiho-shin, Ritual Visits of Deities in Masks and Costumes' on UNESCO's Representative List of the Intangible Cultural Heritage of Humanity (Statement by Foreign Minister Kono)." Press release, November 29, 2018. https://www.mofa.go.jp/press/release/press1e_000105.html.

www.ingramcontent.com/pod-product-compliance
Lightning Source LLC
Chambersburg PA
CBHW070619030426
42337CB00020B/3857